'Do Diff'runt' is Norfolk's quirky motto. This story follows the fortunes of a Norfolk family through the twentieth century. A switchback from poverty to riches, from wealth to obscurity.

It is set where they once lived; in King's Lynn and Thetford. But it moves from the particular to the general. Time passes. People are forgotten.

This is my tribute to idiosyncrasy and courage.

All good wishes to my dear friends Gill and Roy

Anne
XX

Growing a baby only takes nine months. Producing this biography, a 'factionalised' account of my forebears, has taken seven years!

The publication of my first book, 'Day Bugs and Boarders', in 2012, encouraged me to try and capture the rich flavour of my Norfolk family's lives... and here it is!

Anne Culey-Bloomfield, 2019

Previous Publication

Day Bugs and Boarders an autobiography of school life at the East Anglian School for Girls 1945-1953. Still available from the author. £10.99

Please contact the pubisher:

arima publishing
ASK House
Northgate Avenue
Bury St Edmunds
Suffolk
IP32 6BB

(+44) 01284 700321

www.arimapublishing.com

'Do Diff'runt'

Anne Culey-Bloomfield

Published 2019 by arima publishing

www.arimapublishing.com

978-1-84549-752-1

© Anne Culey-Bloomfield 2019

Swirl is an imprint of arima publishing

arima publishing
ASK House, Northgate Avenue
Bury St Edmunds, Suffolk IP32 6BB
t: (+44) 01284 700321

www.arimapublishing.com

List of Contents

Dedication

This book is dedicated; chiefly to the memory of my grandparents and my parents, my husband Jeffrey, who 'held the fort' as I wrote and listened whilst I read it to him, Judi Goodwin and my comrades on the HPB St Brides writing course for their encouragement, my fellow writers in the 'Just Write' group and Vivien Gainsborough-Foot, the friend who always asks about this book's progress.

Thank you all.

A force for good in today's world.

Dear Gill,

Here I'm 'killing lots of birds with one stone'!

Enclosed are;

1) Christmas greetings
2) Diamond wedding invitation
3) the book — out at last!

Hope this isn't presumptious of me to send it but the outlay means I need to recoup funds!

Am doing a presentation at Tiles yard Museum in King's Lynn and another in Thetford.

Much Love,

Anne XX

Jadi .

0033 620384604

Introduction

In the clear light of an East Anglian dawn, the sound of harsh, guttural voices carries over the low lying fen lands. The reeds stir in the breeze and the sad cries of sea birds mingle with the 'thump, thump' of the men's shovels digging into the peaty black soil.

These workers are Walloons from the Low Countries, straightening the Ouse river to make inland navigation possible.

The Duke of Bedford had put up the money, seeking financial reward.

The River Ouse used to be a lazy, loitering river, rising in the Midlands, idling through the low lying counties of Bedfordshire and Cambridgeshire towards Norfolk. Its grey green waters passing through the port of King's Lynn and on towards the Wash and the North Sea through 'the cut'.

The Walloons, the word means 'stranger,' were Huguenots, happy to work in the Fens because they had fled from Catholic persecution.

In cutting a more direct and navigable route to the sea, Lynn became the second most important port in England, proud of its status in trading directly with Germany and Scandinavia as part of the Hanseatic league.

Meanwhile the Walloons stayed on, integrating with the locals in their new homeland, settling close to the Ouse at Thorney, Guyhirn and Tydd Gott. One of these families was named Cueillie, soon anglicised to Culy/Culey. They were my forbears on my paternal side.

The Ouse's tributaries, the Thet and the Little Ouse, mingle at Thetford. The Little Ouse marks the boundary between Norfolk and Suffolk and three hundred years after the Ouse cut was dug by his ancestors, my father moved to live at the spot where the two rivers meet.

From those Flemish settlers to later generations, my Norfolk family had little time to admire the beauty of Lynn town or the great skies above them. They laboured on farms or eeked out a living as inshore fishermen, often near the bread line like most other families in rural communities.

Then, three generations back, they began to diversify, becoming light keepers, publicans, builders, landlords, farmers, cinema and garage owners, restauranteurs and ice cream manufacturers. They'd never heard the word 'entrepreneur'. They just got on and did it, through hard graft, willingness to take a gamble and that stubborn Norfolk urge to "Do Diff'runt".

Chapter One

"Down the Bank"

The light keeper's cottage at the end of 'The Cut', circa 1900

"Cum yew on along a me! Thas toime we were a-gettin on down the point, or the best part o' the day'll go missing!"

During the 1890s and early 1900s, families and courting couples would often take a two mile walk 'down the bank' on a Sunday afternoon. It made a pleasant change from their workaday lives. The path out of Lynn was but an earth path, trodden by generations of 'Linnets', as the inhabitants of King's Lynn were known. It ran alongside the wide, grey Ouse, on top of a grassy bank built to protect the land from flooding. At 'The Point' the walkers could wade onto the marshes, enjoy a picnic or just gaze at the fishing boats and other craft at anchor; for no boats ventured forth upon the Sabbath.

Here people were part of a wide, open vista of sky, water and swaying cow parsley and carpets of bright buttercups. They heard the murmur of insects and above them soaring skylarks called in long sweet skeins of song. Below the bank the constant breeze ruffled the river's surface into wavelets.

The path ended where 'the Cut' flowed into the Wash and here on the point nestled a humble, solitary dwelling; the light keeper's house, let out as a tied cottage by King's Lynn Council.

At that time my great grandfather, John Chase, was living there and my story begins with him.

John Chase was a member of a large fishing family who lived in the closely packed fishermen's cottages known as 'yards' in the North End, a tight knit community with a rough reputation. The North End was close to where their fishing boats were moored in the Fisher Fleet. 'Fleet' was a local name for quay, as in Purfleet. The boats were closely packed near the handsome Customs House.

The hard life of fishermen was made bearable by their sense of comradeship and eased by nightly drinking in the pubs. It was the only release from their daily toil. Most men were worn out by the hard life of a fisherman by the time they reached their forties.

The Chases were large, tough men, renowned for their fiery tempers. They'd often resort to fisticuffs if an argument didn't go their way whilst they were drinking. Nights in the pubs of Lynn must have resembled those Wild West saloons in cowboy films!

One night a fight broke out in the Tilden Smith pub down by the fishing fleet and big Sam Chase, my Grandma's brother, punched his opponent so hard he sent the man flying through a window into the street. Although the glass was smashed it was fortunate the attack took place at ground level or the victim would've suffered worse injuries.

The women had to be tough to keep such men under control. The story used to be told of how John, the father of these rumbustious Chases, was kept in order by his diminutive wife, Rachel, my great grandmother.

The fishing folk used to say "A fisherman without a good wife is like a smack without ballast."

Rachel, formerly Barker, from Holme-next-the-Sea, certainly kept a firm hand on the tiller. She ruled her husband, not 'with a rod of iron' but with a chair leg! If he arrived home rolling drunk from a night at the pub, in the early days of their marriage, she would wallop him, for she was a fervent Methodist and abhorred the 'demon drink'. She certainly inculcated a disapproval for alcohol in her daughters, if not her sons.

Rachel (Barker) Chase and John Chase

It was probably Rachel's influence that led to John Chase applying for a salaried job away from toiling on the sea. She knew that if he applied for the post of light keeper he would receive a regular income and a tied cottage for his family. If he insisted on going to the pub of an evening he would also have a two mile walk along the bank to his home and that would sober him up; if only he could get the job as light keeper!

It seemed a sensible alternative to the cold, back breaking work of sailing a fishing smack, dependent on wind and tides to bring back a catch of cockles, winkles and 'wet' fish such as codlings, thornbacks, dogfish, sprats, and other small fry. In summer the catch would be small brown shrimps which were a great delicacy.

Some of the larger boats headed out towards Iceland for cod but most of the Lynn fleet stuck to inshore fishing, amidst the sand banks of the Wash.

The work became less risky when petrol engined boats were introduced to the fleet. In 1913, Ben Culey, my grandfather, ordered the first one to be built in Lynn. It was sixty foot long and built by Worfolks, the well known firm of boat builders. He proudly named her after his wife and little daughter but this is a long way in the future, as this story begins to unfold.

John Chase, who wanted the job of light keeper, was known to all as 'Sheeper". The pure white curly hair and whiskers that framed his face reminded his mates of a sheep. The fishing community were known for their various nicknames, perhaps to distinguish individuals from others bearing the same surnames. One of his sons, Sam became known as 'Hooker', because he had a large nose. Another fisherman was known as 'Broken Dish' after an unfortunate accident in his home. My Grandmother was called 'Cold Tea' because she always let her cup of tea grow cold. My Grandfather also called her 'Tret' for some unknown reason. Much later he gave me the nickname 'Spinky', because I was scared of spiders.

King's Lynn's Council did appoint John Chase as Light keeper, which was a step up the ladder for him and his family. In 1874 he was paid £36 for his first nine months work, though he had to pay £7 of it as rent for his tied cottage. Even in 1880, six years later, he was only getting £38. 5s for a year's work. Yet he considered this a much better deal than the meagre, unreliable earnings of a fisherman

The estuary lights were essential in guiding the returning fishing smacks safely through the narrow entrance of 'The Cut'. At twilight 'Sheeper Chase' would row across the Ouse, raise a basket containing a bundle of rags and tar to the top of a tall pole and set light to it. Then he would row back across the river to the pole standing near to the point of land beside the cottage and repeat the performance. Every night without fail, come wind or weather.

His responsibilities as a light keeper made him relate in a humble way to all light house keepers, so it isn't surprising that he named his third daughter Grace Darling, in honour of the lighthouse keeper's daughter who rescued sailors from a ship wrecked off the Farne Islands and became a national heroine in 1840.

Gracie was born on October 25th, 1880 and grew up alongside her brothers William John, also known as 'Sheeper', Sam 'Hooker' and sisters Rachel, Sarah and Florence, 'Florrie', in the waterside cottage. She learnt the skills of a fishing lass from her father and became adept at sculling; the art of moving a boat by standing at the back and propelling it through the water, using one long oar in a 'figure of eight' movement.

Imagine the crowds of onlookers gathering along the cut for the annual sculling competition. Everyone was in holiday mood, for a day off from fishing was a rare thing. This was part of the Lynn Riverside Regatta, when the shrimp boats and small fishing smacks also had races.

Grace Darling Chase, the day she won the sculling championship

"Come on Gracie, you ken do 'ut." Her tall, strong brothers are calling to her from the bank. She is tall for a girl of that era and working with her father has made her strong too, even though she's still slender. Grace wields her single oar with ease. Her blue eyes are focussed with determination, her black curls are tossing in the breeze. No wonder she's first across the finishing line to the resounding cheers of the Chase family.

Grace Darling was hailed as sculling champion of the year and had her picture 'took' for the Lynn News and Advertiser. The photo shows her gazing frankly at the camera, proud of her achievement, wearing her own navy blue fisherman's 'gansey', its pattern particular to Lynn fishermen.

The word 'gansey', as it was pronounced in the Norfolk dialect; derived from the island of Guernsey, where the patterns originated. The heavy jumper was made from a tough type of wool which withstood wet and cold. Each port had its own particular design, for the ghoulish reason that a drowned seaman could be identified by the pattern of his guernsey. Few fishermen learnt how to swim and had a fatalistic approach to death at sea.

"If you're stoopid enough to go overboard, that's it!"

Most fishermen believed that the Almighty protected them. Their religious faith sustained them through their lives. Even if they didn't attend a Church service they would never work on a Sunday. Living and working in close proximity they valued the rules, respecting each other's few possessions. It was very rare for them to commit adultery, or to blaspheme, that is 'taking the name of the Lord in vain'. Fishermen's swearing words mostly consisted of adjectives like 'juddy', 'ruddy', 'bloomin' or 'jigger'; and at the worst 'bugger'.

Chapter Two

Grace and Ben

Grace Darling Chase's striking good looks and slim waist soon attracted the attention of male admirers. One of them was Ben Culey, son of David Culey, who had been landlord of the Hop Inn in Church Street before he moved to the Ship Inn, at 13, Queen's Street, Lynn. It was a small ale house, licensed to sell Colchester beer. David also worked as a corn porter to make ends meet; for he had fathered eight children. Benjamin George Culey was the fourth child and had been born on December1st 1878.

It became so difficult for David and his wife Patricia to feed their growing brood that the twin boys who were their seventh and eighth sons were given up for adoption and sent to Scotland, a practice not uncommon in those days of large families and small incomes.

To help the family finances Ben went to work as a house boy for 1/- a week whilst still attending St Margaret's Primary School. At fourteen years old he was sent to work full time at Trenowath's, a corn merchant, in Norfolk Street.

Ben would say with pride, "I could shift a sixteen stone bag of corn on my back, or carry two hundred weight of cotton cake seeds; you know, the sort used to feed cattle".

He stayed at Trenowath's for twenty years, all the while building up his own business ventures.

With his links to the fisher folk of the North End he was able to start his own fish merchant's business, sending fish daily by train to the London markets. His acumen and instinct for a wager soon had him buying up cottages at auctions and selling them on again by nightfall at a profit, all conducted with a shake of the hand, no solicitors, no estate agents involved. At one time he became an undertaker and then a coal merchant. Once when a circus was in town he even bought an elephant... just for a lark.

This is how Ben, the poor boy, became Ben the business man. Now he was in a position to pay court to the comely Grace Darling. At the end of a day's work he could often be seen making his way 'down the bank' to visit her and win her over with his quick wit and mischievous twinkling eyes.

Benjamin George Culey in the Volunteers before 1900. He was a drummer.

When I was young I would often be told the tale of how another suitor got to hear of young Ben's wooing. He knew the times he visited the little cottage and lay in wait for him behind a hawthorn bush. Ben strides along the narrow path, signalling his approach loudly, as he whistles a happy tune, glad at the prospect of seeing his Gracie again.

The jealous rival jumps out and confronts him.

He raises a shot gun to his shoulder.

Ben ducks his head and swerves to the left. Fortunately he is nifty on his feet.

In his agitation the assailant misses hitting Ben, the bullet goes over his head, just missing his skull.

In a second Ben recovers his balance.

With a strong right hook, for he's done a bit of boxing in the Volunteer reserves, he sets about the other fellow, knocking him straight down the bank and into the squelching mud of the Ouse.

Then he unloads the gun and chucks it after his rival.

The man is humiliated. No other action is needed on the part of Ben.

If Ben hadn't been so quick witted, the course of this history might have been different!

The lovely Grace decided that Ben was the right man for her and they were married on June 4th 1900 in St Nicholas Chapel, where Grace's father, Grandfather and Great Grandfather were also married. There are no grave stones commemorating this long connection with the church, for poor fishing folk were not deemed worthy of note and unable to afford memorials.

St Nicholas Chapel

Though St Nicholas was built as a Chapel of Ease; a resting place for the dead, it is better known as the Fishermen's Chapel. This beautiful, lofty church, with the longest nave of any Chapel of Ease, has a tall spire that acted as a landmark for returning seamen. Sadly, because of the cost of upkeep, it is now a redundant church, cared for by the Church Conservation Society. People with connections to the fishing community can still be baptised, married or have their funerals there. Because it has such a high ceiling with excellent acoustics, concerts take place there during the King's Lynn Festival each summer.

But let us get back to the happy couple, Grace and Ben, setting out on their one day honeymoon. They travelled to Hunstanton, a burgeoning seaside resort founded by the Le Strange family and known locally as 'Hunston'. It was only fifteen miles away. Ben had hired a horse and cart for the day. No expense spared. Unfortunately they didn't know that the carrier was a heavy drinker and the horse stopped at every single pub along the route.

Ben commented, "I had a juddy lot o' trouble makin' him move. The hoss wuz used to a long wait outside all the pubs. I din' know the ole feller was a drunk."

From that brief honeymoon ensued fifty three years of loving marriage; interspersed with fights, for they were both people of strong will and hot temper. There were arguments as to whose turn it was to get the dinner; Ben loved cooking, rows about their three children, about Ben's liking for alcohol, all the usual ups and downs of a lifetime partnership.

When I stayed with them as a child I would often hear bursts of laughter coming from their bedroom, as they snuggled into the depths of their feather mattress, supposing they were hidden from the listening child by the thick curtains of their four poster bed.

On their Golden Wedding morning I remember the annoyance of Granddad when a posy of yellow roses arrived for Grace. The card read "from an old admirer".

"Who's sending you flowers?" burst out Granddad. A tempestuous row ensued. As a naive fourteen year old I was amazed that an old person felt jealousy so strongly at such a great age and yet I felt touched that Ben's darling Grace still meant so much to him.

Who could have sent those roses? Might they perhaps have come from the spurned suitor who was such a bad shot all those years ago? I never did know but my Grandma was certainly still a charmer and could be very gracious, even though she had become quite stout with the passing years, due to good hearty food and being driven everywhere by Bill, their chauffeur and general factotum.

Chapter Three

Starting Out

At first Ben and Grace lived at 1, Loke Road, close to their families. 'Loke' means lane in the Norfolk dialect. Ben kept a small general stores there. Their first child, Mabel Evelyn; 'little Evelyn' as Grace always called her, was born in 1904 and was baptized at St Nicholas on 14th December 1904. In the four years since their marriage Grace had suffered several miscarriages, so Evelyn must have brought joy to their hearts. Alas, they lost this child too, because when she was but two and a half years old, Evelyn developed diphtheria and died.

Grace was expecting her second child at the time she lost Evelyn. It would have been hard to manage her grief at any time for a dead child but her emotions must have been even more complicated by the fact that she was heavily pregnant with the coming baby. Unfortunately this was a tragedy suffered by many families before the days of vaccinations.

I remember asking about the gold locket Grandma wore around her neck, suspended by a delicate chain. Even all those years later, tears filled her pale blue eyes, as she showed me the little twist of golden hair inside, a keepsake of her lost daughter.

Grace Darling tableau, collecting for the Lifeboat. Ben is wearing a white panama hat.

On the August Bank Holiday of 1906 Ben Culey arranged a tableau of Grace Darling, played by his own darling. She stood in a boat with a well known character of the North End, 'Duggie' Carter beside her. The cart was pulled by six Lynn fishermen, two of her brothers amongst them. It was a money raising effort for life saving apparatus, as part of the National Lifeboats Appeal. The cart moved slowly along the streets, strong fishermen in their Sunday best 'gansays', held long poles with nets on the end, to collect money from the crowd and from people watching in the first floor windows of houses.

Just over a year later Grace and Ben's first son came into the world on a wild winter's night; November 15th 1907. He was christened Benjamin Chase Culey. The first son in a family was usually called after his father, often with his mother's maiden surname as a middle name. Benjamin inherited his mother's blue eyes and her hot temper. He also inherited his father's 'go getting' attitude to business but of course that was not apparent for some time. Although in childhood he had dark brown curls like his mother, his father's genes disposed him to start losing his hair in his twenties; his answer to this early baldness always being, "Grass doesn't grow on a busy street!"

A sturdy little boy, Bennie, for his name was quickly abbreviated, often provoked his mother by his stubborness and he told me how, if he was defiant, he would be tied to the bed post and given a beating with a belt.

"If Mother was riled with me"

Small wonder then, that this boy, who later became my father, sometimes resorted to similar treatment in the raising of an equally strong willed child; though Daddy would most likely use his hand to spank me on the bottom. The firm disciplining of children was considered essential as a means for adults to stay in control, an unquestioned response to childish bad behaviour, which dated back to a time when there were numbers of youngsters growing up in crowded conditions, alongside a tired, work weary mother and father. The traditional stern disciplining of children was evident at the dinner table, for when we were with my grandparents I would be admonished by my Granddad, only half in jest that, "Little girls should be seen and not heard."

Another piece of advice was; "Look with your eyes, listen with your ears but keep your mouth shut."

Bennie was joined in 1910 by his brother, John Edwin Valdemar Culey, although 'joined' does not accurately describe their volatile, combative relationship. Johnny's exotic name 'Valdemar' was a nod to the boys' Uncle, who was Danish.

This uncle, Valdemar Andersen, had been a marine surveyor and sea captain but having been dubbed the black sheep of his family in Denmark after a tremendous quarrel with them, he'd landed up in Lynn, where he had acquired a shipping agency and also Florence, known as 'Florrie', as his wife. She was Grace's equally strong minded sister, known for loudly voicing forthright opinions. Despite frequent ructions within the partnership they produced two very blond, good looking youngsters. Then Valdemar became ill and not trusting English doctors to cure him, he returned to Denmark, maybe to escape the argumentative Florrie? His trust in Scandinavian medicine did not produce a cure. He died, leaving his wife and two children fatherless, on this side of the North Sea.

John Edwin Valdemar was, according to my father, the favourite child. Certainly Grace seems to have been more indulgent towards him. It was always 'my Johnny' when she referred to him; Just 'Bennie', when she talked about her elder son.

John was certainly the handsome, blue eyed boy, resembling a young Frank Sinatra or Kevin Costner in his lean and hungry looks. But whereas Bennie was growing up to inherit the 'go getting' character of his Dad, Johnny was inclined to coast along, relying on his looks and the easy life he had at home, as his parents grew more affluent.

Bennie went happily to St James Primary School, thirsty for knowledge. A hint of his later gift for making speeches came when he was awarded a gold sovereign at the age of 10 for a political talk on "What I would do if I won the election."

By 1917 Grace and Ben were really prospering, through owning and also renting several farms. They had moved to a large property, formerly the farm house of Folly Farm. They called it Folly House, and retained some of the farmland as an extensive garden. Ben set about modernising it from the rather square, plain building it had been, into a spacious and comfortable home. The house was situated about two miles from the centre of Lynn on the Wootton Road, which leads northwards towards Hunstanton, in the area called Gaywood. At that time it was being developed as an affluent suburb of Lynn.

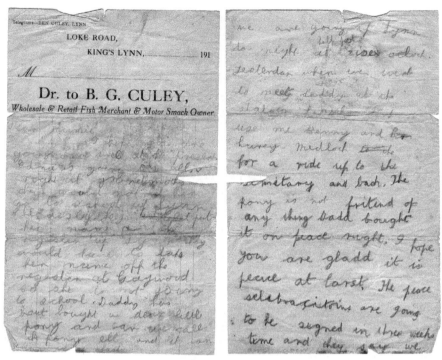

An early letter to his mother mentions the end of The Great War.

Lynn had grown rapidly during Edwardian times because of the opening of the Alexandra and Bentick 'wet' docks in the 1890s, which enabled larger ships to dock in Lynn. The docks linked to the railway system and opened up job opportunities in the expanding town.

Meanwhile Bennie and then Johnny went on to King Edward VI Grammar School, where Bennie did well, having a curiosity about the world and a mind that absorbed facts. With their gift for sociability and generosity Ben and Grace Culey, with the headmaster, Mr Rayner and some teachers, took boys from King Edward VI Grammar School to a Summer Camp at Carisbrooke Castle, on the Isle of Wight. It was a good holiday for boys who might not have otherwise had such an opportunity and the arrangement continued long after Bennie and Johnny had left school.

Edna, Bennie and Johnny circa 1917

Chapter Four

Bennie sets sail

"The more we live, more brief appears
  our life's succeeding stages,
  A day in childhood seems a year
  and years like passing ages" - Thomas Campbell

Bennie was angry and disappointed when his father announced that he should leave school before Matriculation, the equivalent of 'A' levels in those days. He'd shown academic promise and had ambitions to become an engineer.

"I always wanted to build bridges' he would say with a sigh in later years. He deeply regretted his father not allowing him to stay and get a 'sustificate' as he called it.

Of course, in the long run, being an optimistic kind of chap, thwarted ambition didn't get him down. He put his imagination to good use in the design of cinemas and houses, without any paper qualifications.

He was one of those men who designed things 'on the back of an envelope'.

His Dad's response to matriculation and then further education had been, "You've learnt as much as you'll need."

His father, with a business man's nose for results, saw only that it was costing him £10 a year to keep Bennie at school. There was also Johnny to pay for as well.

Enough was enough.

So Bennie was sent to work at the King's Lynn Sugar Beet factory, where he tested sugar beet for sugar content, as an assistant analytical chemist.

Ben, remembering how he'd started with nothing and how hard he'd had to work to improve his prospects, thought to himself, "Is all that juddy Grammar School education really necessary?"

How strange that years later Bennie's daughter's future almost foundered on the same premise. When it was suggested that I should aim for University, my father's reply to the Headmistress of my school was;

"It'll be a waste of time for her to go to University when she'll most likely marry a farmer."

I didn't marry a farmer, only an impoverished minister. Though I had a teacher's certificate, through my own determination to get to College, Daddy thought being his secretary would suffice as a job.

After giving birth to three daughters I still thirsted for knowledge and thanks to the Open University I funded my own way through University!

But let us return to Bennie, aged seventeen in 1924, who has been sent off to earn his keep at the sugar beet factory.

The astute Ben Culey had sound motives for installing young Bennie there.

When the lorries carrying the beet from the Culey farms delivered it to the factory Bennie got to know and on his father's advice set it aside for a few hours to dry out, before testing it for the sugar content. This meant the sugar percentage was higher and his father got a better price for his crop. Just one example of the native cunning that had made Ben a successful business man.

Bennie worked twelve hours a day, seven days a week through the season, even working eighteen hours when changing from the day to the night shift. There were no regular breaks for meals. Bennie was also responsible for providing First Aid for three hundred men if it was needed. For all this he received £3 a week which was considered good pay at the time.

At last, and with great relief, Bennie was sent as an assistant farm manager to his Dad's farms at Marham and Narborough. One field was huge, over 600 acres, and at the time it was the biggest field in Norfolk. As Bennie said, "Even on the ruddy tractor it took half an hour to plough from one side of the field to the other!"

The Marham farm was later sold to the Air Ministry and developed as an aerodrome, later evolving into the huge air station it has now become. In doing so the name underwent a change. Older Norfolk people called the village 'Marram', as in Marram grass, but to the RAF and USAF personnel it has become MAR-ham.

As well as using Ford tractors about the farms, Bennie had taught himself to drive a car by practicing on the rough farm tracks. There were no driving tests in those days.

There were few leisure hours for Bennie but with the vibrancy and tenacity of youth he found time to join the tennis club; shoot pheasants, often 'poached' from the Sandringham Estate, go on swimming parties to Hunstanton and in quieter moments keep up with his oil painting and violin practice.

Through his love of music he met his first love, Kathleen Prior, who lived across the road from Folly House. Bennie played his violin whilst Kathleen accompanied him on the piano and soon romance began to blossom. Grace, outspoken in her likes and dislikes, loudly disapproved of Kathleen, "She don't enjoy her food". A sin in a household where food played a Rabelaisian part in socialising. Grace also condemned Kathleen for being uppity; another sin, for Grace and Ben had never lost the common touch and kept their friends from the North End, even when they prospered and formed other friendships.

With the loud disapproval of his mother, young Bennie's first romance was sharply nipped in the bud.

Close knit communities tend to relay news in a manner similar to jungle drums and so, through news from someone in Lynn, Bennie, in his seventies, heard that his first sweetheart Kathleen, who had married and moved to Fenstanton in Cambridgeshire, had just lost her husband. He decided to pay her one last visit, "For old times sake," he said to his wife. And wisely she decided to accompany him there.

Chapter Five

More about Johnny

At this point we leave Bennie, managing his first farm and return to his siblings, Johnny and Edna.

When Johnny finished at the Grammar School Ben arranged for his second son to take on the management of the Majestic cinema in Lynn. Later he managed the Capitol cinema, which his father had built in Hunstanton and then the Pilot Cinema in Lynn, which opened in 1938.

Johnny was finely built and good looking. Girls were attracted to him. Olive Maltby had marked him out as 'a good catch' as soon as she'd met him. Olive had a peroxide perm and a tinkly little voice. She had cultivated a simpering manner which irritated Grace and enchanted Johnny. Her father owned a fish and chip shop but the smell offended Olive and she worked at WH Smiths.

John and Olive

Olive, in Grace's words, "gave herself airs." Like many mothers, Grace often didn't approve of her sons' choice of girl friends. From all that I heard there were doubts as to whether Olive would be the steadying influence that Johnny needed.

Whilst a house was being built for them on Wootton Road; within easy reach and perhaps the control of his parents, they lived at Folly House. Grace, of course, disapproved of Olive's flimsy underwear.

"Wisps of material, no bigger than a handkerchief" Grace would grumble, as the delicate objects fluttered on the line beside Grace's voluminous celanese bloomers.

Johnny did not have Bennie's grit or determination and was more dependent on his parents to provide for him. At that time he lacked the will to choose his own path in life and he didn't take his work as cinema manager all that seriously.

Bennie resented the fact that his younger brother had been given much more financial help than himself.

Wedding of John Edwin Valdemar Culey and Olive Maltby. 1934

When war against Nazi Germany was finally declared in September 1939 Johnny's parents were worried that he might be conscripted into the armed forces, as cinema management was not a protected occupation.

Johnny was indeed called up for military service but he had the makings of a very reluctant hero. He was scared; his wife was distraught at the idea of being left alone and his mother was in great distress at the thought of her Johnny going away to war.

What was to be done? How would they manage without their boy? He was plagued by their anxiety and his own fears.

As a result something appalling occurred.

Johnny went into an empty garage at Folly House and locked the door.

A shot rang out. It broke the quiet of a sleepy afternoon. Grace and Bridgie, the housekeeper, ran into the yard. Loud, anguished cries could be heard from inside the garage. They rattled the door and called for Johnny's father, who had to force the door open. There, huddled in a corner was Johnny, his shoes and trouser bottoms soaked in blood, which was still oozing onto the dusty floor. His face was contorted with pain. By his side was one of the shotguns used for killing rabbits, pheasants and foxes on the farms.

"Johnny, Johnny, oh what have you done!" wailed Grace, whilst Bridgie covered her face with her apron and wept, for she couldn't help being fond of the feckless young man. Grace quickly took control and despatched Bridgie to phone for an ambulance. The bullet was removed in hospital.

Rather than be conscripted Johnny had shot himself in the foot, so that he wouldn't pass the medical. The smashed foot repaired in time but the damage done was not only physical.

Oh, the ignominy of it! How shameful for the family!

His brother Bennie was particularly disgusted. He classed his brother as 'a coward'. Bennie, a farmer, was in a reserved occupation and therefore could not leave the land but he believed it was his duty to fight if necessary. He couldn't understand how Johnny could stoop so low to avoid serving his country. The police must have asked questions about the incident but no action was taken and Johnny was declared "unfit for military service". Later it would be spoken about as "an accident on the farm" but the unpleasant incident put an even further distance between the brothers.

In the following years Johnny caused his parents further heartache. There were rows about money, for Johnny never thought he was paid enough and his parents were concerned about his lackadaisical interest in the cinemas.

As a child I received a single present from my Uncle John and Aunt Olive. It was a book of Aesop's Fables; tales of low cunning, avarice and cowardice, expressed through animals' behaviour. As an adult I realised it had been quite an appropriate present from this couple.

They didn't like children or want any of their own.

"I think having children might spoil my figure" twittered Olive to her sister-in-law, my mother.

Eventually Johnny and his fragile wife decamped to Bournemouth on the South Coast, putting an even greater distance between themselves and his parents than Bennie was to do. But this was an emotional as well as a physical distance. There had been a major bust-up. Once again it was about money. The separation grieved his mother deeply, though I sensed that my Granddad was glad to see the back of him.

Grandma's missing him was understandable, even though he had become a source of constant pain to them both. It always seems to be the absent son or daughter who is yearned for and who becomes the favourite; not the steady one, who is there to offer constant support to ageing parents through the weeks, months, years of their remaining lives.

Johnny and Olive did not come to either Ben or Grace's funeral, though Johnny turned up when there was a sale of house contents, before Folly House was put on the market. He had already written to his brother Ben, listing the items he wanted which were, of course, the best pieces. Johnny was steely eyed and grim faced.

"I've come for my share of the furniture" he sneered.

He'd ordered a van to take the furniture away and demanded a cash settlement after the sale of the house, although the price it fetched didn't even cover the death duties. Then he b......d off back to Bournemouth without bothering to visit his sister, Edna.

A few years later when I was staying in Bournemouth on holiday, I looked him up in the phone book and turned up at his photographer's shop to satisfy my curiosity. I hadn't told my parents that I might call on him in case they tried to stop me.

Uncle John was very surprised and not at all pleased to see me, even though I'd had nothing to do with past disagreements. We spoke for a few seconds whilst he fiddled with an expensive camera. He promised to phone the bed and breakfast place where I was staying, to invite my cousin and me to his home. As we pulled open the plate glass door to leave he called after us, "Get free of the family as soon as you can!"

He did phone that evening but his message was brief.

"It's not really convenient for you to come round."

This innocuous rebuff felt like a slap in the face.

There was no further contact with John.

Some years later we learnt, after he'd died, that for a considerable amount of time he'd been treated in hospital for schizophrenia. This revelation helped us at long last to feel sympathy for John and Olive.

Chapter Six

The Sad Tale of Edna May

Edna May was Ben and Grace's only surviving daughter and this is her story.

Edna tucked her cotton frock into her knickers before she waded into the surf.

The wind at her back whipped her dark curls into her eyes, so that she strained to catch sight of the small ghostly shrimps she was herding into the wide shrimping net. She screwed her eyes against the bright sun and used all her childish strength to push the heavy wooden shaft through the ruffled shadows of the incoming tide.

After a while she was exhausted and with relief she heard her brother's voice carried on the wind.

"Hev yew got a fair ole ketch, Edna gal?" Bennie called as he slip-slided down the shingle bank to help her.

"Dew yew leave me be" she spat at him. "Oi ken dew ut." But he only laughed at her wilfulness and emptied the wriggling mass of shrimps into the pail he'd brought, setting off up the steep bank to their summer home with Edna stumbling in his wake.

Bennie, Edna May, Grace Darling, Johnny and Benjamin George Culey at Heacham. 1915

'Boston Seas' was a bungalow, a ramshackle construction of two railway carriages serving as bedrooms and a large central living area and kitchen.

This makeshift home was where the Culey family decamped from King's Lynn each summer, from a house of generous Edwardian proportions to rustic simplicity.

Bennie, Johnny and Edna washed their catch free of sand at the outside tap and their mother Grace boiled the shrimps in a pot on the stove. The family sat round the scrubbed pine table tearing off the paper thin shells, stuffing the sweet juicy shrimps into their mouths, supplemented with cockles and whelks; but never mussels in those days, for mussels were considered 'dirty feeders', as they feasted on sewage, which in those days was emptied straight into the sea from waste pipes.

Edna May was the fourth and last child of Grace and Ben. Born in 1913, early photos show a pleasant child with a round, open face framed with dark curls. Grace was so happy to welcome another little daughter into the world, having lost her first to diphtheria.

Grace with her daughter Edna

Not long after this particular summer holiday Edna was diagnosed with epilepsy and her carefree life changed. The fear and uncertainty of occasional 'fits' led Grace to mollycoddle her daughter. A nursemaid, Mrs Bridges, affectionately known to all as 'Bridgie', was appointed to watch over Edna. The little girl was constantly watched. Her clothes were chosen for her, she wasn't allowed to attend school and wasn't even encouraged to brush her own hair. Consequently Edna, unlike most women of the family, stopped thinking for herself and lost the will to become independent of her doting mother.

"Come on now Edna," Grace would say.

"I've asked Bill (the chauffeur) to bring the Bentley round. You and me are going up Lynn to buy you new shoes".

"I like these ones, they're comfy," Edna would wail.

"No they in't. They can't be 'cos they hev a grit big hole in the bottom."

So the thirty year old woman would be cajoled to leave the sofa and she and her seventy year old mother would be driven the two miles to Kirks shoe shop in the High Street because Edna was oblivious of the holes in her worn out shoes and too lazy to do anything about changing them on her own.

Because her parents felt sorry for her, Edna found that if she took a fancy to something she could make a fuss and get it.

Once, when she was about twenty years old her Dad was going to Heacham to 'do a bit of business' and took Edna along for the ride.

She took a fancy to some of the pretty little bantams in the Bradfield's back yard and lunged forward to catch one. In her haste and clumsiness she fell against a glass cucumber frame, shattering the glass.

"Now look what you've ruddy well done!" grumbled her Dad.

He paid for the damage but Edna, unrepentant for her clumsiness, kept begging for the bantams until her Dad paid for those as well and Edna took them home triumphantly.

Later on in life, when she might have known better, she coveted my Scottish Terrier, 'Mac' whom I loved dearly. I was about ten years old at the time and he was the first dog that was actually 'mine'. I had chosen him as a tiny black scrap.

I had trained him, fed him and walked him. It shocked me to the quick that he could be taken away from me, handed over to Edna without anyone sparing a thought as to how the change would affect him, let alone me.

My Grandma had asked Daddy for him, "Edna's taken a fancy to him and you know, he'd be company for Edna. After all, Anne is away at boarding school for a lot of the time"

I thought this particularly cruel. After all, I'd lost my dolls and my pony. Was I now to give up my cherished dog?

This was the way Edna deployed others to get what she wanted. She was altogether a disappointing Aunt, for her idea of fun was to jeer at me and mimic the way I pronounced words. Having been sent to boarding school Daddy had paid extra for me to have elocution lessons, "So that you can talk proper, Anne."

I'd soon learnt that cloaking my Norfolk accent prevented me from being teased as a 'swede' or country bumpkin.

But at Folly House Aunt Edna would mimic the way I said 'Varse' instead of 'Vawse' or 'Thearter' instead of 'the-ater'. Maybe she was jealous that I had managed to cope with being away from home, for she'd never had a chance to grow up in any real sense.

By the time she was in her thirties her parents were worried as to who would look after her when they died.

"What will become of Edna when we're no longer here? Bridgie's getting too old, we can't reckon on her now".

No man had ever shown interest in Edna. She had become idle and grown fat from over eating.

"Mornin' Mister Cooley. I unnerstan yew hev sum wark fer me?"

Percy Barlow had come to Folly House to do some building jobs.

A bluff country chap, red faced, with a loud laugh and bad teeth, Grace soon noticed how often she'd find her daughter sneaking out to chat with him whilst he worked. Glancing through the kitchen window Grace was amused to see her daughter's body convulsed by giggles and not by one of her 'fits'. Percy's guffaws filled the yard, he was obviously flattered by Edna's enjoyment of his silly jokes. They seemed easy and comfortable together.

Despite Percy's high colour, signalling his fondness for the bottle, Ben wasn't particularly worried. He liked a drop of drink himself and viewed non-drinkers with suspicion as 'milksops'.

Percy was a farm labourer who'd done some jobs for them before, so they reckoned he'd be a steady worker.

A deal was struck; a bungalow purchased and some hard cash settled on Percy to ensure he'd marry their daughter. In other words they'd 'bought' Edna a husband.

Percy and Edna's wedding, St Nicholas' Church

It was not so much Percy's drinking but his other pastime, gambling, that later confirmed to them both that their choice of Percy as a suitable husband, had been a mistake.

The wedding gifts, so tastefully displayed after the wedding in 'Glendalough', the bungalow in Marsh Lane that Ben had bought for the couple, gradually disappeared, one by one, to feed Percy's gambling habit. Then other things, paintings, jewellery and china made their way to the Lynn pawnshops.

Though Percy was put out by Edna's uselessness in keeping their home clean and in her lack of care in her appearance, he stayed with her. In colloquial terms he knew 'which side his bread was buttered.'

Edna daydreamed about those happy childhood days at 'Boston Seas' in Heacham.

43

"See that little finger sticking up out o' the Wash over there, my booty? Thass Boston stump, the tower of St Botolph's Church. In Boston, Lincolnshire."

Alas, Edna knew the high tides of the great sea surge in 1953 had battered their seaside home 'Boston Seas', tearing it apart and sweeping it out to sea.

Time had wrecked Edna too. She developed diabetes and although the ulcers on her legs throbbed painfully, she managed to get to her niece's wedding in 1960.

"So glad you could come, Edna," said Ben's wife, trying not to screw her nose up at the unwashed smell emanating from her sister in law. The change she saw in Edna was shocking. Though only fifty one years old she looked like an old woman.

Not long after the wedding there was a phone call from Percy.

"Hello, B-b-ben." He was blubbing and could scarcely get out the words.

"E-e-edna passed away th-this mornin. Ken yew cum over? I dunt know wot ter dew."

The state of the bungalow appalled Ben and he stifled a sob. Dust lay thick on the dilapidated furniture. The electric bulbs hung on bare cables. Half empty tins of mouldering food had been discarded in the living room. The smell of decay hung heavy in the air. The tattered curtains were drawn across the windows but in the gloom Ben saw mice skittering boldly across the filthy carpet, their tiny feet leaving delicate footprints in the grime. Everything of value had been sold long ago.

At the Registrar's Office Ben handed in Edna's death certificate. The cause of death was given as "Diabetes and Senility." A sad end to his sister's life.

Percy stayed on in the bungalow, but though he'd inherited what was left of Grace's jewellery he soon sold it to fund his addiction to gambling. He too wasted away, amongst the broken, dirty furniture, the peeling wallpaper, the ceilings draped with cobwebs.

Sozzled by drink and emaciated by lack of food, Percy died alone. Neighbours alerted the police after there had been no sight of him for a week. When the police broke down the door of the bungalow they found him lying amongst the ruins of his 'home'.

I inherited their bungalow. Fortunately this had been written into my Grandmother's will, so that Percy couldn't get rid of it to his own advantage.

"It'll never sell," said my father, looking at the neglect and damage it had suffered over the years.

After we'd had it repaired and decorated it did sell and I was glad to be rid of a place with such sad memories.

An unhappy chapter but part of the weft and weave of this Norfolk family.

Have I been biased in my account of my father's brother and sister? To be honest I have only recorded what I saw and heard as a child. I sensed the anguish they caused their parents and also my father, their elder brother.

Chapter Seven

The Road to Love

With a sense of relief let us now return to the story of our young 'hero'.

By 1928 Bennie, now twenty one years old, was considered by his Dad to have had enough farm experience to manage a farm on his own and so he was sent to the nearby village of Middleton. Ben Culey was renting Manor Farm there, which belonged to the well known Gurney family.

It was the time of the Depression and cattle raising was in the doldrums. There were no subsidies to help farmers through tough times and Bennie was making minimal profits on the raising of cattle. He was supplying meat to his Dad's butcher's shop at 6, Saturday Market Place and supplying the General Stores at 60, Loke Road, which had been put in Bennie's name.

Always with an eye to advertising Bennie had printed free ink blotters for customers; "Blot out your troubles and buy your meat from us!'

Hector Prior worked in the butcher's shop and eventually bought it, so then the name changed to 'Priors'.

Bennie was a sociable fellow and he got very lonely in the big farmhouse, with only his liver and white spaniel, Bess, for company. He drove into Lynn as often as he could in his spare time.

Johnny and Bennie still enjoyed motoring to the tennis club and having a match or two with whoever was there. At that time there weren't many families in Lynn who could afford to buy or maintain a motor car, so two good looking young men with a car would have found favour with the female players.

Whether they caught the eyes of a particular couple of young ladies or whether it was the young ladies who first took notice of them, it's hard to say.

The young ladies in question were Grace and Cassandra, who was known familiarly as Cassie. Their father was William White, and they lived at St Nicholas House, St Nicholas Street, Lynn.

The sisters were well known in the town. Not for any questionable reasons but simply because of their striking, almost Spanish, good looks. They both had glossy raven hair and were the first in Lynn to have their hair cut short in a modern 'bob'. They adopted knee length dresses in the 'flapper style', wore white, rather than the more prevalent black stockings and were seen about town in the very latest styles of the Jazz Age. They often wore matching outfits, which they or their mother had made at home.

Gracie and Cassie White with their mother.

People turned to look at them and wondered if Gracie and Cassie were twins, for their similar looks and because they always went about together. They followed their mother in having good fashion sense. I wonder how their strict father regarded this unseemly devotion to fashion?

Bennie and Johnny knew the girls a little by chatting to them at the tennis club.

One Sunday afternoon the young men were cruising around Lynn in Bennie's car and saw the girls walking just ahead of them on the pavement.

They drew up beside them and Bennie stopped the car.

"Hello Miss White," he called to Cassie, whose arm was linked through Gracie's.

He probably addressed his greeting to Cassie because she was the bolder of the two. Although Grace was older, she was rather shy and kept her eyes down.

"Would you care to come for a spin with us on this lovely afternoon?"

Whilst he was talking, Bennie was surreptitiously taking a look at another young woman, who was hanging back, half hidden by Cassie, as she chatted to him.

Bennie continued, "I see you've got a friend with you today. Would she like to come along too?"

"Ooh" laughed Cassie, "That's not our friend, that's our sister Jessie;" adding unnecessarily, "She's older than us. I don't s'pose you've seen her at the tennis club? She works at Kirk's shoe shop during the week."

Bennie nudged his brother hard to get him out from the seat beside him.

"Righty ho," he said. "Well now, Cassie, you and Miss Grace get up in the back with John and you, Miss, come up here in the front with me."

And that was how my mother and father met.

Why had Bennie taken such a sudden liking to Jessie, in preference to the dark eyed beauties, Grace and Cassie? She had soft brown hair, azure coloured eyes and a pale complexion. In fact colouring similar to his own.

He was often heard to explain his preference by saying, "It was her blue eyes and gentle ways what done it!"

That afternoon's drive was the start of a journey which lasted seventy two years. Bennie described it by harking back to his times at the Tennis Club.

"The score was Love-----All"

Grace and Jessie, Hunstanton 1928

Chapter Eight

Meet the Whites

And now it's time to tell you more about the Whites, Jessie's family.

Her mother, Jessie Maud Osborne, was born in 1883, the daughter of a shepherd, who worked for a farmer on Knights' Hill, just north of Lynn. Jessie Maud had attended school in Castle Rising, where she had learnt fine sewing and thus gained a position as a lady's maid in the household of the Barclays, a 'County' family. This stood her in good stead later on, when she sewed her daughters' beautifully made dresses and instilled in them a sense of fashion.

On her mother's side Jessie was related to the Suckling family and through them to the famous Norfolk hero, Horatio Nelson; for Nelson's mother's youngest brother William, was her forebear. Jessie had inherited the same fine aquiline nose that Nelson had and if anyone had popped a bicorne hat on her head, the resemblance would have been quite startling.

William White's father, Thomas, had been an active member at St John's Parish Church, where even the Vicar referred to him as 'a saint'. William, born in 1882, became a member of the Plymouth Brethren in his youth, which meant he adhered to a more austere style of life. William had served an apprenticeship as a carpenter and later called himself a master builder, for he had built two fine houses. One still stands on the left hand side of the Setchey Road leading out of Lynn, near the Hardwicke roundabout. Despite his rule of abstinence, in 1905 he also built a public house, 'The Flowerpot', on the corner of Chapel Street and Norfolk Street. Like many of the other buildings in this family story, it has been demolished.

Most of his livelihood was in carpentry; sheds, greenhouses and other necessary wooden articles.

Jessie and William were married in August 1904 at Castle Rising Church.

Afterwards Jessie, coming from a more easy going family, had to adjust to the frugal, austere lifestyle that William followed.

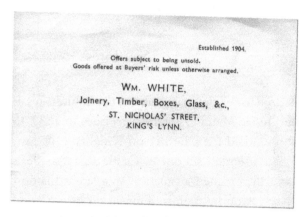

Established 1904.
Offers subject to being unsold.
Goods offered at Buyers' risk unless otherwise arranged.

WM. WHITE,
Joinery, Timber, Boxes, Glass, &c.,
ST. NICHOLAS' STREET,
KING'S LYNN.

Letter head for William's carpentry busines.

At first they lived in Austen Street but when the carpentry business prospered, they moved to St Nicholas House, a larger property at the junction of St Nicholas Street, Austen Street and St Ann's Street.

St Nicholas House, home of the White family.

Meals were plain and served on the scrubbed pine table. A small joint on Sunday would be eked out, so that slices could be served cold on Monday and even used for cottage pie on Tuesday. Potatoes were plain boiled. Pudding would be stewed fruit without custard and maybe a water biscuit. Tap water was the only drink available.

The kitchen was dark with a butler sink, a cheap gas stove and no other facilities. There was an outside lavatory and no bathroom.

Although William listened to the six o'clock news, when 'the wireless' became widely available, the radio was never used for the frivolous purpose of entertainment. After the news it would be switched off for the

52

rest of the evening and the wooden shutters on the tall windows would be closed.

William would put on his steel rimmed reading glasses and read the Bible for half an hour, during which time everyone kept quiet. His religious observance did not extend to congregational worship. It was a private matter. He shunned doctors and medicines, and every ailment was treated by the little white pills of arnica or other simple methods of self medication.

The theatre and cinema were considered idle pursuits and bad language and alcohol were banned from his house.

Family life centred around a small fire in the grate. On one wall was a large faded print of the famous Victorian painting by Landseer 'The Monarch of the Glen', showing a red deer in the Highlands of Scotland. On another wall were family wedding photos set into oak frames made by William White. Displayed prominently on a shelf was a large glass case containing a sailing ship.

"That was made by my father, Thomas White," William would say with pride.

Thomas, before he'd settled down to work at the Docks and regular attendance at St John's had been a mariner.

"He sailed three times round the Horn."

William spoke with pride, for he regarded this as a considerable achievement on the part of his father.

Cape Horn, a rocky promontory at the cold southern tip of South America, is a notoriously turbulent coast, where the waters of the Pacific and the Atlantic clash and mingle. Its wild winds and dangerous rip tides have been the graveyard of many ships.

There were never many visitors to the house on the corner, for William didn't hold with entertaining; though close family members might be offered a cup of tea and sometimes a biscuit.

The lighter touch of Jessie's personality was hardly present in the home, except for the large green aspidistra plant on the sideboard and the wooden biscuit barrel with its well polished silver lid, which had been a wedding present.

No wonder that Jessie and her daughters enjoyed watching people as they passed by the tall window. They shared gossip about the lives of the various passers by.

Jessie radiated good humour and even after they had married her daughters would travel to Lynn to be with her every Tuesday, which was market day in Lynn.

Despite William's rule of austerity in the home, the Whites, like a few other prospering families in Lynn, including the Culeys, embraced motoring before it became widely used as a means of transport. The family visited the far flung corners of the British Isles; John O'Groats in the far north of Scotland, Land's End in Cornwall and a trip to Yorkshire, just for the curiosity of seeing a total eclipse of the sun. All were recorded in the family photo album.

The White family out in their 'Swift' motor car.

Although William's way of life was rigid, rather surprisingly he taught his daughters to drive the car and in the early 1930s Cassie and Gracie had saved enough to buy a 'bull nose' Morris motor car, which gave them the independence to travel about on their own.

The Whites by then were prosperous enough to rent a house in Hunstanton near the sea front and they spent summer holidays there each year.

Gracie, Cassie, William, Jessie (Mother) and Jessie (eldest daughter)
Holidaying at Hunstanton

The paved yard at the back of St Nicholas' house was stocked with piles of freshly sawn wood. William had a branding iron with his mark inscribed WW. At the docks he would stamp the wood he'd bought and it would be delivered to the work shop by horse and cart. The Alexandra dock, where wood from Scandinavia was unloaded was but a short walk from the house and in time he would ask his little grand daughters to walk there with him when they visited.

Timber arriving by horse and cart

With a small hand tucked firmly into his gnarled bony fist the child would trot along side. Often they would sing the hymn "There is a green hill far away" as they walked, for this was his favourite. I don't think my grandfather knew any popular songs. On the way back he would slip a half crown into the small damp palm and say;

"That's for being a good girl"

Though what each grand daughter had done to merit this unusual generosity never became clear.

The high stacks of wood exuded the rich pine smell that transported William in imagination to the deep silent forests of Sweden. His workshop was redolent with the fresh smell. Sawn wood always conjures up in my mind the sight of the man, busy in his workshop, wearing his long brown overall, an old brown trilby clamped firmly onto his head above his thin, pinched features, his stern countenance belying the tender feelings he had for his family.

The purpose of the ever present trilby was to hide his bald head. William had suffered from alopecia as a child and had lost all his hair, eyebrows and eyelashes.

He usually wore a wig but it was so old and discoloured to a rusty brown shade, that it didn't resemble natural hair at all.

Jessie Maud Mabel was born on June 19th 1906, a year after William and his wife were married. She was christened in St Nicholas Chapel, just across the road. The Vicar stood close to the font, holding the small bundle of baby in the crook of his arm and intoned, "Name this child,"

The Godmother answered "Jessie Maud" then quickly added her own name, "Mabel".

William shot a withering look at Mabel, annoyed at her presumption but it was too late. Jessie had three names, not two and so when another daughter was born she also had to have three names. Grace Harriet Hannah was not the last daughter, for Cassandra arrived in 1910. She was rather grandly named after one of the Barclay girls; the family that had employed Jessie before her marriage. This one fanciful name was deemed sufficient. Cassandra was proud of her unusual name, although it was inevitably shortened to Cassie. When the time came for each of the three girls to start school they were sent to Thoresby College, a small private school for young ladies.

It was not till 1913 that the longed for son was born.

My mother, the eldest girl used to tell me, "I used to be given the task of keeping an eye on my younger sisters as well as Willie in his pram.

My brother was only a few months old when something terrible happened.

Cassie and Gracie were running ahead of me. I was calling out and trying to catch up with them, as I pushed Willy but there was a big stone on the path and I didn't see it. The pram tipped right up and Willie went flying out of it in a bundle of shawls and blankets.

Now look what you made me do, running off like that I said, as Willie burst into tears. I picked him up quickly but he wasn't hurt. Thank goodness that all the clothing broke his fall."

The two other girls were sworn to secrecy, so William and Jessie never knew what happened to their precious son that day.

William's eldest daughter, my mother, Jessie, started work at Kirks, a shoe shop on the High Street. The daughters of middle class tradespeople were not expected to pursue a career. But taking a small job until they got married and became the responsibility of their husband was considered 'respectable'.

The White sisters were known from an early age as keen followers of fashion and many heads turned to view the trio as they strolled down the High Street, arm in arm. They remained very close to each other, even after marriage and it was noted by their daughters that when they referred to each other they would always say, "I'm going to see my sister Cassie (or Gracie)" or "I'm going to see Mother." Never "I'm going to visit your Auntie Cassie/Gracie" or "I'm going to see your Grandma".

I found this hurtful because it seemed to set a distance between me and the close ties between my mother and her family. I felt this more keenly because I didn't have any sisters of my own.

When Jessie worked at Kirks she was a modest young lady and so prone to teasing by young men who fancied her. One of the male shop assistants tried his luck.

"Do you like birds, Miss White?" he enquired one day.

"Of course I do" Jessie replied, "Why do you ask?"

"Well then, how about a little lark with me?" The artful young man quipped, with a knowing wink.

Jessie, blushing furiously, hurriedly retreated to the store room and busied herself amongst the shoe boxes, trying to avoid him for the rest of the day.

Her father must have got to hear of this because shortly afterwards he told Jessie to give in her notice and come home to help her mother.

She had another admirer, nicknamed by her sisters 'Wonk Winkley', although his real name was Frank Masters. Did he walk with a limp or did he have a turn in his eye? I've often wondered.

Nicknames were prevalent in those times and 'Bennie' Culey hated the use of his babyish name by the family, which distinguished him from his father. One of the reasons he liked Jessie was that she called him 'Ben' from the beginning of their friendship.

Chapter Nine

Bennie pursues his dream

Jessie Maud White, aged 22

Jessie may have had one or two early admirers but it was young Bennie
Culey who began courting her seriously, even though he was only twenty
years old.

He wooed her with the enthusiasm he always had for a new project.
She was soon taken to Folly House to meet his parents, for he wanted to
show her off and have their approval at the same time. Fortunately Grace
approved of the quiet, modest, well mannered young woman, whilst his
father liked her looks. With a twinkle in his boot-button brown eyes, he
was soon greeting her visits in typical Culey fashion.

"Whoops the girl Jess,"

He'd exclaim, as she entered the room.

Bennie, with low cunning, set out to test her, just as he'd tested the sugar content of the beet. Was she as sweet as she seemed?

One day whilst out for a walk they found shelter under a tree during a sudden shower of rain. Jessie was wearing a new, very fetching cloche hat, dusky pink and trimmed with silk roses. She didn't want to get it wet.

Wickedly, Bennie reached up and shook the branch above them. A torrent of raindrops drenched them both, spattering upon Jessie's new hat and her coat.

He'd done this on purpose to see how she'd re-act. Most women would rightly have been very annoyed but wise Jessie just laughed at the silly prank and took the joke in good part. This attitude stood her in good stead in years to come, when Ben was dead set on pursuing some crack pot scheme. Hers was the quiet voice of reason that acted as a brake on some of his impetuous schemes.

Following this episode, Bennie was convinced that Jessie would make a good wife. He telephoned St Nicholas House to make an appointment to see her father; then he dressed in his best suit and tie, slicked down his unruly hair and drove to the austere grey house of Jessie's family.

He banged the big iron knocker and fidgeted nervously on the scrubbed white doorstep.

William himself came to the door and peered down at the youngster standing there.

"Mr White, I'd like to marry your daughter,"

Bennie blurted it out, before he could stop himself.

Now of course, William had been appraised of the young man's intent by his wife and daughters. He knew the Culeys to be a well to do family with flourishing businesses all over the local area but he was not sure whether he approved of them and their life style; so different from the one he'd imposed upon his own family.

Silently and reluctantly he led young Bennie into the sparsely furnished living room. The youngster noticed it was nothing like the opulent and comfortable surroundings he was used to at home.

William might have opened the door across the hall; to the more richly furnished parlour, with its Victorian wallpaper and upright piano but this special room was reserved for important days, such as Sunday afternoons or Christmas.

No, this young whipper snapper could be interviewed in the more ordinary living room. Unbeknown to William White, his wife and daughters were huddled at the top of the stairs, attempting to catch the conversation drifting up from below. William White spoke sternly.

"I've heard you're managing one of your Father's farms now but you're still very young. I don't know if you can look after my daughter properly. If you're really thinking of marrying Jessie, come back in a year's time when you've reached twenty one years of age. Then I'll know if you are sincere in your intent."

Bennie was stunned. Before he could respond, William was leading the way back to the hall.

It felt such a rebuff to the ardent young man.

Jessie's father opened the front door, held it ajar for Bennie to leave and quickly shut it.

William had doubts about the reliability of one who could make decisions so quickly about marriage and doubted the suitability of Bennie Culey as a husband for his precious eldest daughter.

Jessie and William White

Chapter Ten

Life at Folly House

Whilst William White is left wondering whether a match with the Culeys would be the best thing for his daughter, let's take the two mile walk towards Gaywood, where Lynn is expanding in an affluent ribbon development; along the Wootton Road to Folly House, formerly Folly Farm. Here we'll take a look at the Culey's way of life, for William White is right; their style of life is very different to his own, in fact the contrast is quite overwhelming.

When I was old enough to be aware of the difference in life styles I preferred to walk and not ride the distance in a car because it gave me a chance to adjust to contrasting ways of life and living. As I gained social awareness I realised that the household at Folly House was like a Chekhov play; with a large cast of characters and laughter, mixed together with the buzz and banter associated with the plays of the quick witted Oscar Wilde.

The other household at St Nicholas House had something of the grimness of an Ibsen play, where emotions were kept under control or even repressed and other people's lives continually reviewed and criticised as the sole means of entertainment for the females of the household.

At Folly House there was a welcoming, Bacchanalian atmosphere. Tradesmen who called or workers doing jobs there, would be invited to sit down with the family at 'dinner', the main meal of the day, which happened around three pm. The timing of dinner was a throw back to Grace's upbringing within the fishing community, when boats had unloaded their catch of fish. As with labourers on the fields of Norfolk, work began early in the morning and by three pm people were hungry for food. Days ended with the coming of darkness, for lighting cost money. Although this was no longer a problem for the Culeys, now they were financially secure, they maintained the eating patterns of their forbears.

The long mahogany table would be set with heavy quality cutlery and crowded with steaming dishes of meat and vegetables. Their favourite was a hearty stew, floating with 'swimmers,' the Norfolk name for large floury dumplings, that filled hungry stomachs. Often a large suet pudding would be cooked in a cloth in the copper.

Ben was renowned for his 'swimmers,' flavoured with herbs and bits of meat. However his family loved reminding him about the time a lady guest was taken ill after eating one, clutching her stomach and complaining of stomach cramps.

"Quick, look sharp! Phone the Doctor. She's gorn pale... her breathing in't right"

The doctor bustled in, commanding everyone to step back and not to crowd the poor woman. After a quick examination he announced,

"She'll have to go to hospital. I'll call an ambulance."

Next morning her husband rang.

"Just to let you know... Florrie's OK. It weren't Ben's cooking! It were 'pendicitis and she's had it out!"

For years afterwards Ben was teased about how;

"That woman ended up in 'ospital after eatin' one a' yore swimmers".

Ben loved to cook and often there would be a tussle with Grace as to who would cook the next meal.

One morning Grace confronted Ben, as he sat smoking his pipe beside the sitting room fire.

"You've been and killed three of my rabbits for the pot, haven't you?"

Ben feigned ignorance,

"No I hent."

"Oh yes you hev. I've just been out doors and the rabbit shed door's open and one of the cages is empty and there's blood on the kitchen floor."

Ben knew it was no good denying it. He'd been caught out good and proper and he owned up

"I thought you'd like a bit of rabbit for dinner, Trett." he said, trying to soften her up by using his pet name for her.

"Huh," said Grace. "Well, I 'on't get nothin' for the fur now, will I?" and she stormed off. Grace in a stormy mood could be very intimidating.

Every Saturday Ben would head off to Lynn Walks, to see Lynn play football. He sat on the front bench, next to his chum, Lynn's MP, Mr Wise.

Ben instigated an annual football game for the Culey Cup, between Wisbech and King's Lynn. It was a huge silver trophy that was stolen at one time but later recovered and returned to the club.

After the football game Ben returned home to high tea and the nation's football results were read out over the radio on a Saturday evening and Ben and Grace checked them against the predictions they had made in the 'Pink 'Un' newspaper. There would often be shellfish for tea, including winkles, which were teased out with a pin.

The Culeys loved 'dressing up'.
Here is Grace Darling 'reading' Jessie White's palm by the Culey caravan.

The girls at the table would take the small brown closures used to seal the winkle's mouth and stick it on their cheeks, as if it was a beauty spot.

Then other members of the large family would turn up to play 'Nap' a game of cards. Bottles of beer would be fetched; the cards were shuffled and small bets of sixpence or a shilling, a 'bob', would be made on the result. Later there would be singing round the piano or listening to records on the gramophone. Grace's favourite was 'Whispering' Jack Smith; though she was partial to all male 'crooners'.

As the effect of the beer and port wine took hold, there would be charades, when Grace's wardrobe and chests of drawers would be raided for costumes and the scenes could get bawdy.

Was it any wonder that the two families viewed each other with suspicion?

Grace Culey and Jessie White could have become friends, for they were both generous of spirit and liked fun. But their husbands were poles apart.

William White was regarded as mean and penny pinching by the Culeys, whilst he regarded their household with suspicion, almost as a 'nest of vipers'. He considered them too easy going, too hedonistic. I can't recall ever seeing either couple entering the other's home.

Grace always avowed in public,

"Ooh, I never touch alcohol"

This was out of respect for her feisty little mother, Rachel, who had attended the Methodist Chapel in the North End and had 'taken the pledge' not to drink liquor. Rachel Chase brought her daughters up not to touch the stuff, even though she had less success with her roistering sons.

Ben liked a drop of whisky and would hide bottles in the grandfather clock and in odd corners around the house, so that Grace wouldn't know how much he was drinking, Grace, on the other hand would reach into the capacious sideboard if she thought no-one was looking and bring out the gin bottle to pour herself a 'nip', whilst she settled down to read 'The Christian Herald,' licking her forefinger to turn the page. When she'd finished she would get out the peppermint cordial and take a good sip of that, so that no one could smell spirit on her breath!

The folk at Folly House were fun loving, generous, rumbustious and often stormily argumentative; they lived life to the full and the people of Lynn liked them for it.

The Culey/Chase Family having fun at Hunstanton.

Chapter Eleven

If at first you don't succeed...

Ben Junior had inherited the persistence and drive of his Dad, so on the evening of November 15th, 1928, he gathered his courage and, heart thumping, once again rapped the iron knocker on the front door of St Nicholas' House. As the stern William opened the door he blurted out;

"Good evening, Mr White. Today I've turned twenty one and I'm here to ask for the hand of Jessie in marriage."

Out of his pocket he drew a box and flipped it open to reveal an emerald and diamond engagement ring, which he'd bought at Harrods, a prestigious department store in London. Although this action quite amused William, for it looked as if Ben was presenting the ring to him; he typically stifled the smile that was forming on his thin lips and, taking young Ben into the parlour this time, reluctantly agreed that an engagement could be announced; but with one more proviso.

"Oh, and what is that?" the ardent young suitor enquired.

William insisted that the couple should remain engaged until June 1930, when Jessie would be twenty four and old enough in her father's eyes, "To know her own mind."

Ben was furious. He felt he had waited long enough for the consummation of his dreams.

It was only by exerting the forcefulness associated with his future business enterprises that he eventually got his future Father-in-law to agree to an earlier date. That is why it was a winter, rather than a summer wedding and a date was set for January, 1930.

It is the case in even the most equable families that tensions build with the differing perceptions of a wedding and with two very disparate families there were lots of disagreements.

As the father of the bride and with two other daughters' weddings to fund in the future, William was minded to be careful with the expenditure. It was expected that after the wedding in St Nicholas Church there would be a quiet gathering at the bride's home, before the couple set off on their honeymoon.

Grace and Ben expected to give their eldest son a right royal send off, with a big reception and an evening dance at the Majestic Ballroom, which was situated above the cinema. Ben Culey senior told William that he was quite prepared to fund this part of the day himself. William was stubborn. He didn't want a lot of 'show'.

In the end the Culey's held out for having an evening party and they paid for it. They generously let the Whites have the pretty little engraved champagne bowls as a present afterwards; but William and Jessie White stayed away from the dance. The Culeys didn't understand their attitude and were hurt by their absence. Needless to say the younger generation had a jolly good time.

The champagne glasses remained hidden and unused until they were passed down to the White grandchildren.

It was an endearing trait of the Culey family that gifts were given at the slightest opportunity. No-one left Folly House empty handed. An innocuous comment such as;

"That's a pretty vase," ('vorse' as it was pronounced in Norfolk) meant that Grace would immediately scoop up the object and press it into the hands of the surprised visitor. Quite a lot of her cherished possessions found their way to other homes in Lynn.

Ben and Jessie bought their wedding china at Scotts, in Lynn's High Street and their furniture at Ladymans, a Lynn department store. In those days it was the practice to give a complimentary present after a good order and so Ben and Jessie received a chrome standard lamp with an ebony stepped base, bearing a chrome frog, very much in the Art Deco style. It has remained in the family over the years, with various changes of lampshade reflecting the changing styles of interior design.

Although it was but a short step across the road from her home to the church, it was not the practice to walk to one's wedding, so on January 30th 1930, Jessie arrived in a carriage drawn by a pair of 'greys', as white horses are known amongst the equine fraternity.

The bride wore a modest dress of cream moire velvet with a long simple veil held in place by a circlet of wax orange blossom. She carried a sheaf of arum lilies. This was very much the look of a 1920s wedding.

As Jessie alighted from the carriage, one of the arum lilies caught in the door and so when the couple arrived at Goodchilds for their formal photographs, Jessie looks disgruntled because of the broken lily stem. Ben stands slightly apart from her, very serious on his wedding day.

The sisters, Gracie and Cassie were bridesmaids and wore dark red moire velvet, as befitted the winter weather. Edna had not been asked to be a bridesmaid. Could this omission have added to the tension between the families?

The Wedding of Ben and Jessie
Cassie White, John Culey, Ben, Jessie and Grace White

How glad the couple must have been to get away!

It was dark and snowing heavily, so they only got as far as Cambridge on the first night, for an unscheduled stop in a disappointing hotel. Maybe they were nervous too, because they spent their first evening as a married couple by going to the cinema.

They moved on next morning to London, for the rest of the week's honeymoon.

Not used to driving in London, Ben was horrified when a London 'Bobby' stepped into the road, firmly holding up his hand in a gesture requiring Ben to stop the car. He was going the wrong way up a one-way street!

Ben rolled down the driver's window in trepidation and was bawled out for his infringement of the law.

"Sorry, Officer" he responded, quite humbly for Ben, "I'm just up from the country. I'm on my honeymoon."

The policeman looked down at the young man. He doubted that this laddie was a "country bumpkin." The young man's cheek in trying to fool him didn't go down well.

"I'll make him sweat" he thought to himself, holding back for a second or two. Then he slowly put the pencil and note book back into his breast pocket.

"All right son," he muttered "I won't book you this time but perhaps you'd better be getting back to where you belong?"

With relief Ben put the car into gear and drove onwards, a very nervous Jessie beside him.

Then, after a week of 'seeing the sights' in London, they drove back to the beginning of their life together in Norfolk.

Jessie and Ben, Great Yarmouth, 1930

Chapter Twelve

Stormy Weather

"You can always tell a Norfolk man, but you can't tell him much!" - Sidney Grapes

Life at Manor Farm was not easy for the new wife. Jessie had never lived away from her close knit family. Now she was expected to take on the chores of farm life and Ben expected her to spend what little leisure time they had with his family. It was a tussle of wills and Ben usually won.

Jessie and Ben, Manor Farm, Middleton

The Great Depression of the 1930s affected farming in East Anglia. Beef cattle were fetching ever lower prices. Ben was buying in Irish stock at £17. 10 shillings a head, feeding them up and selling them fat for £22. 10 shillings, which was a poor profit margin. The farms at Marham, Yarborough and now Middleton had lost about £20,000. The start of their married life was a very difficult time for the young couple and as the worries about income increased, tension mounted and there were arguments.

One morning, after a disagreement about money, Jessie felt she could take no more.

She was crying bitter tears as she packed a small suitcase. Ben had left the farmhouse to feed the animals. She put on her coat, took one look at the breakfast dishes in the sink and closed the door behind her.

Ben returned to a silent farmhouse. The spaniel Bess looked up mournfully from her basket, not even bothering to come to the door to give him her usual welcome.

A note was propped up against the teapot.

"Dear Ben,

I didn't think our life together would be like this. I can't take it. Sorry, I'm going home.

Jessie."

"But THIS is your home" Ben cried out to the empty house around him. For once the man of action didn't know what to do. He had wooed and won his precious Jessie and now she'd left him. She'd not even written 'love' at the end of the note.

Ben with Bess the spaniel

Meanwhile back at the White's house Jessie was sobbing her heart out, as she recounted to her mother and sisters how different life was from what she thought it would be. Cheery Ben had turned into a short tempered, angry man.

72

Her father was not sympathetic.

"You were sure you wanted to marry him. It's too soon to give up. When things are tough a wife must stick by her husband. You can stay here for a while but your place is with him."

It was a long speech for William. Because he was a man of few words when he did speak, his utterances mattered. Jessie felt in her heart he might be right and felt duly chastened.

Ben did not rush over to Lynn and harangue his wife to return. His pride was hurt. Instead he phoned her every day, begging her to come back, reminding her that her real 'home' was with him and their future path was together.

After ten days Jessie felt ready to return and with relief Ben drove up to St Nicholas House to fetch her home.

When Jessie saw him, his face was pale and drawn. He hadn't been sleeping. She could see the little vein twitching beneath his right eye, as it did if he was anxious. She came forward very slowly and uncertainly. Then he put his arms round her and hugged her tight. Oh the dear, familiar scent of him. She thought to herself "I'll never leave him again." And she never did.

Whilst they were apart he'd had time to think and a new plan was taking shape.

The concern about Jessie and her sudden departure made Ben realise what was really important. He needed to break free from the emotional and financial hold his parents had over him and he knew that Jessie too, might benefit if she was not under the influence of her father.

One evening when the day's work is done, Ben and Jessie are sitting in the kitchen at Manor Farm. Bess the spaniel is nuzzling her head against Ben's tweed plus fours.

"I've been thinking" he begins.

In a year of married life, Jessie's already learnt that Ben's 'thinking' signals change and perhaps trouble ahead.

Ben continues, "We can't go on like this; losing money on the cattle, scraping a living, worrying about money all the time."

Jessie sighs "But what else can we do?"

Ben sets out his plan. He's already decided drastic action is needed.

"We need to move away. Cut our links with farming (and family)" he adds to himself.

"My father has always decided what I should do. I'm twenty four. Time I struck out on my own."

Chapter 13

The story of Gracie and Cassie

Grace beside the bullnosed Morris that she and Cassie bought in 1932.

Whilst Jessie and Ben are contemplating a new future, let us briefly return to the other White girls and see what happens in their lives.

Gracie, the second daughter led a more sheltered life than her elder sister. She did not get the chance to work away from home. Gracie was not even sent to school until Cassie was of an age to start.

My mother, Jessie, would tartly dismiss Gracie's years at school by saying;

"Gracie was never much good at book learning."

This can't be verified. I do know that Gracie had a mild, sweet disposition.

Gracie outside St Nicholas Chapel with Bess

She met her husband to be, Lewis Means, at the Kit Kat Club in Hunstanton. Once Grace and Cassie had bought their 'bull nosed' Morris, they had the freedom of the open road.

Gracie and Lewis married on February 27th 1935 and it is interesting to see how fashions had changed since Jessie's wedding in 1930. Gracie's wedding attendants, Jessie and Cassie, wear glamorous fish tailed satin dresses and hold satin muffs in the style of Hollywood stars. Gracie holds an enormous bouquet, nearly as big as herself and she wears a long veil.

Gracie's Wedding, 1935

But after such a stylish wedding, Gracie's life hereafter was of a spartan nature. If her sister Jessie had found married life a challenge, living away from her close knit family, it must have been even more so for Gracie, for she started married life in the quite primitive conditions that existed on Fenland farms.

Lewis took his bride to the family farm. Officially called Marsh Meadow farm, it was familiarly known as 'Banks of Clay', It stood by one of the fenland 'drains', dug to drain the land of water and to help prevent flooding of the precious black peaty soil.

Water had to be pumped up by hand for all household purposes, the lavatory was an earth closet and there was no electricity, so in the evening paraffin lamps would be lit. Only open fires warmed the rooms and those rooms could be very damp in that low lying countryside.

As a child I liked the differences between my modern, centrally heated home near a town centre and the remote farm where my cousins lived. Chickens would be running around in the yard and we could play on the haystacks and slide down them, catching pieces of straw in our hair, whilst our bare legs would be scratched by the rough stalks.

In the sitting room there was a typical 1930s suite with tassels on the arms and we played one of the few records 'We want a little white room with a window by the sea' over and over on the wind up gramophone, until Aunt Gracie would tell us to stop.

Ben had given her that gramophone for her 21st birthday and it was one of her treasured possessions.

Farming was a struggle and there were two daughters to support. Margaret Grace was born on 27th October 1936 and Bridget was born on July 11th 1943, after Gracie had suffered several mis-carriages. Later in life Lewis and Gracie gave up the farm and moved to Emneth. They had a small holding in the village, growing raspberries for the commercial market. It was a hard life for my favourite aunt but I never heard her complain.

Cassandra was more feisty and strong willed.

"She should have been a boy" her father would say.

Cassie had a head for figures and worked in Lloyds Bank in Lynn's High Street until she was 'called up' to serve her country, during World War Two.

Cassie at Hunstanton looking 'stylish'

Cassie decided to join the WRNS known as the 'Wrens', the female branch of the Navy.

Typically it was a choice based on Cassie's sense of fashion, for she admitted,

"It was because I liked the uniform". Did she maybe hope a handsome sailor might pass her way? She looked so attractive in her uniform.

Unfortunately Cassie was sent to the remote wildness of Bodmin Moor in Cornwall, where the Wrens' headquarters was in a bleak building called 'Glynn House'. Not only was Cassie unsuited to the hard discipline of life in the Forces but she became ill with pneumonia and was eventually discharged for health reasons. One of her father's letters to her shows the humanity of this outwardly austere man.

Like many other women of her age Cassie lost her sweetheart, the dashing young soldier, Jock, who proposed marriage to her shortly before he went to war and was killed on the battlefield.

Cassie 1936

It was years after the war had finished that Cassie finally married her long time boyfriend, Robert Appleton, who had been in the RAF. On returning home he had moved back to his childhood home to care for his invalid, widowed mother. Only in 1953 did Cassie persuade him that she could share in this care. At last they were married and Mrs Appleton senior came to live with them until she died. The gentle, good natured Bob, who had seen distinguished service during the war, was welcomed by the nieces as their new 'Uncle' and the couple shared years of quiet happiness together; spending their final years in a residential home in Hunstanton.

Cassie and Bob's wedding at St Nicholas Chapel 1953

Chapter Fourteen

The Black Sheep of the White family

"What is to be done about Willie?"...a familiar question uttered in turn by the three sisters, Jessie, Gracie or Cassie, as a response to the latest indiscretion of their errant brother.

If Johnny and Edna were a worry to their parents, it was as nothing to the consternation caused by Willie to his prim and proper father, his soft hearted mother, his sisters and the women in his rackety life!

Willie was born in May 1914 and at first joy abounded, for he was the longed for son, successor to the wood merchant's business. There were two parents to attend to his needs and three 'big' sisters to pet and spoil him. Adulation was bad for the growing lad. It led him to expect attention from all quarters, especially as he grew into a good looking boy, blessed with thick, glossy raven hair and melting dark eyes like Gracie and Cassie.

William Jr. with the family's Swift motor car

He was sure that he was the centre of the universe!

His high opinion of himself was gained from frequently gazing at himself in the little cracked mirror hanging in the kitchen. So not only did he grow up vain but also selfish, putting himself first, in whatever he did.

Willie as a young man

Early on he shrugged off the austere religious observances of his father. The bright lights of a provincial town held the lure of searchlights for him. After a tiresome day working beside his father he would escape from the house. Like the fellow in 'Under Milk Wood' he could have been nicknamed 'Up to no good boyo!'"

When Willie is about twenty an angry father is banging on the door of St Nicholas House. Father William opens the door, taken aback by the insistent heavy knocking.

The man outside, clad in a heavy tweed overcoat, deerstalker hat pulled well down over his ears against the cold rain, shouts belligerently, "Now see here. I've come about your son."

"You'd better come in out of the wet" William says, looking nervously up and down the street to see if anyone has heard the man's angry voice.

"Huh" the man grunts, as he steps in, dripping pools of water from his thick coat onto the hall floor. "I'm not bothered by the rain. I'm bothered about your son. He's got my daughter in the family way."

William is taken aback. Nonplussed. Could it be true?

"What do you mean? Not our Willie? Are you sure it's him?"

"Oh yes. my daughter told me. She don't know anyone else... So, what are you going to do about it then?"

The man stands in the small dark hall, fists clenched, desperately trying to rein in his fury.

The mild mannered, upright William leads the man into the living room, where Jessie has been listening; appalled at the revelation.

Willie wouldn't have known anything about contraception and abortion was a dark mystery.

After further talks between the two sets of parents, Willie was summoned to a meeting of both parents and firmly told that he must do the 'right' thing. . That is, to marry the girl.

It was a very quiet wedding at Freebridge, for the girl lived on the Royal Sandringham Estate. Indeed, her father was Clerk to the King. He hadn't been able to keep his daughter safe. Like the royal pheasants roaming the grounds she had been 'fair game' to the predatory Willie.

There was a daughter from the union but as it was only whispered about in corners, the three grand daughters were not privy to full knowledge, so the details are hazy. "Not in front of the children" was a saying that carried weight in this family. Trained to be correct and proper, under the influence of a strict father the sisters had carried a burden of loyalty towards a brother who behaved badly and yet whose misdemeanours should not be talked about openly. Mere grandchildren could only piece together small pieces of the jigsaw. We surmised the marriage didn't last.

Willie, not noticeably chastened by the failure of his marriage after just one year; continued in the workshop, making boxes, wooden frames, sheds and so on.

Around five he would have tea prepared by his mother and then spruce himself up in the kitchen, which doubled as bathroom, smooth down his thick hair, play with the luxuriant moustache, cultivated in the belief it made him even more irresistible to young women, then take himself off to the Dukes Head Hotel on the Tuesday Market Place; where he would prop up the bar, make himself out to be a fine fellow to anyone fool enough to listen to his opinions and eye up any attractive young ladies there, in the company of their male companions.

The rascally Willie

At home he would sometimes escape into the parlour where he played the piano.

Never having had a formal lesson, his hands would wander up and down the keys in a meaningless river of sound, in much the same way as his wandering hands would play upon any young woman flattered by his seductive conversation Around 1947 he somehow managed to gain the affections of a classy, sophisticated young woman who lived in the leafy, affluent Home Counties. Her name was Margaret, nicknamed 'Garry'.

The wedding in Surrey was a good day out for the White family, although looking at the photograph it is noticeable that the bride didn't wear white. Perhaps she had been married before and had lost her first husband in the war? Perhaps it had to be a Registry Office wedding as William was divorced?

The wedding in Surrey
Ben, Jessie and William White, Willie, Gary and Cassie on the far right

84

The secrets around Willie's life thickened like fog as time passed. The marriage to Garry didn't last either. She left him for a Major and they ran a hotel in Mundesley for some years.

On Jessie and William's mantelpiece there was a photo of a little girl with a round face, dark bob and dark eyes gazing down at her cousins, who never had their photos up there.

When I asked Mummy,

"Who is that little girl?" she replied in a whisper,

"That's Elizabeth, but you mustn't ask questions about her."

And so the secrets continued.

Willie's daughter Elizabeth

"What about Willie?" The sisters murmured in hushed voices. There was always some fresh gossip circulating in Lynn about him.

As we grew older my cousins and I began to speculate about Uncle Willie, as 'the skeleton in the cupboard', although Willie was getting more rotund as the years passed and not at all like a 'skeleton. '

One afternoon when Mummy and I called to see Grandma, there was a new born baby lying on the living room table, having his nappy changed, whilst a young woman cooed over him.

"This is Wee Willy Winky'" she purred, as she happily fussed over the little boy. I had never seen her before and was not told who she was. I never saw her or the baby again.

Such mysteries made me wonder if I had imagined this whole episode, yet the memory has stayed with me and even though I was young, I thought that this innocent child might be another product of Uncle Willie's insatiable appetites.

The family business was failing now because Grandad was becoming frail and more dependant on Willie's efforts to keep things going but William was not dependable. He made no effort to get new orders and sustain the business. He had never had much interest in it. Through Willie's lack of effort and interest his father was eventually declared bankrupt. The ultimate humiliation for such a conscientious man.

Strangely, William's eldest sister,. Jessie, continued to be loyal to him, holding on to the picture of him as the little boy she'd accidentally tipped out of his pram.

Grace and Cassie tended to sympathise with the women he had wronged. They had lost respect for him.

After his parents died Willie continued to live in the sad, neglected house. He tore the wedding photos out of their surrounds, so that he could sell the fine oak frames to an antique dealer. He sold the model of the sailing ship in its glass case, made by his grandfather Thomas and also the huge family Bible, so treasured by his father. The funds fuelled his habit of visiting the Duke's Head bar every evening.

"Can I buy you a drink?" he would murmur, having caught the eye of a young woman.

Once he was properly caught out,

"No thanks, I've heard about you and actually I think I'm related to you" one girl said, as she quickly moved to another part of the lounge.

In the end he was too sick and ill to dress in the silk lined suits he'd bought from Goddards of Lynn. Too frail to walk to the Duke's Head hotel any longer.

His legs were ulcerous and an odorous smell seeped through the bandages.

The three sisters held a cabinet meeting.

Cassie said "I can't be responsible for him any more"

Gracie added "I don't see why you should, just because you live the nearest."

Jessie, who still felt the most kindly disposed towards her brother, put in a plea, "Well, with Mother we each looked after her for three months at a time."

Cassie cut in quickly "No, no, we can't do that, he'd be too much of a liability".

She'd had enough of looking after her own mother and Bob's mother too.

So they decided that Willie would have to go into hospital for treatment.

However, it was too late to save him. The only thing the sisters could do was to fiercely defend his privacy during the last weeks of his life; keeping away the few people that might have visited him, ashamed of the diagnosis that had been given.

Willie died of syphilis at the age of seventy, a full twenty years before his older siblings passed away.

"How lovely the flowers are," I whispered to my cousins, as we processed down the long aisle of St Nicholas' Chapel at his funeral.

"Yes, the flower decorations are ready for the King's Lynn Festival. It's taking place this week." Bridget said.

"Granddad White would've approved" I commented. Smiling to myself, I remembered how our maternal Granddad could be so careful with money and how he would have appreciated not having to pay for the funeral's floral arrangements.

The house had been remortgaged and so it came into the possession of the Council and was renovated by the King's Lynn Trust for the preservation of interesting properties. It was renamed White's House, which stands as some kind of memorial to the family.

Chapter Fifteen

'Fresh Fields and Pastures New'

We left Ben and Jessie contemplating a new direction for their life together. Was it Ben's intention to move to another part of the country or perhaps to emigrate? Some of his mother's family had gone to America and settled in Oregon at the start of the century, so that might have been a possibility for the young couple?

No. Nothing as drastic as that. They were only looking to move to the Ancient Borough of Thetford, thirty miles south east of Lynn.

In the 1930s when few people had cars or moved away from the place where they were born, that would have seemed quite a significant decision.

Thetford at that time was a small market town of some 4,000 people, surrounded by the largest lowland pine forest in the British Isles, planted by the Forestry Commission in 1910 and covering an area of 80 square miles. It was begun as a project to anchor the sandy soil and provide wood for ships and pit props for mining.

Although Thetford was still in Norfolk, the distance from Lynn was enough to give the couple the independence Ben craved.

'The People's Picture Palace' was too grand a title for the ramshackle wooden cinema that Ben was thinking of buying. Not long before this children could gain entrance by the collection of jam jars as an admission fee. The People's Palace only showed silent films and 'the talkies' were coming in. So Ben needed to get his business off on a good footing.

Considering that celluloid film was so highly combustible, the juxtaposition of a building constructed entirely of wood and the nightly use of flammable film in the projection box, could be a dangerous combination of materials.

The cinema had already suffered damage by fire when the owner, Mr John G Brown of Vicarage Road, had put it up for sale.

The People's Picture Palace after damage by fire.

"I don't think there's a future in 'talkies'" he confided to young Ben Culey.

How wrong he was!

Ben was ready to stake his future both on 'talkies' and the cinema business. He had a vision of bringing the world, through the medium of entertainment, to this small town.

Ben Senior wondered if the venture wasn't the height of folly but whilst he regretted his son's decision to move away, Ben was magnanimous and shrewd enough to invest in this 'dream'. Together with Mr Allflatt, a Lynn builder, they offered to get Ben Junior started with a loan. Mr Ernest Adams of Ripley House, Lynn acted as a guarantor.

First of all, though, Ben and Jessie had to find somewhere to live.

In 1931 there were only two houses for sale in Thetford. One was 'Lyndhurst', 51, Croxton Road, next to the railway line, at £440 and Fern House, in Earl Street, selling for £875. Ben and Jessie, especially Jessie, were cautious.

"We don't even know if we'll like Thetford well enough to stay for long" said Ben, whilst Jessie thought to herself,

"Better not spend too much on a house, when we're in debt to his father."

So they settled on the smaller house, though no doubt Ben drove a bargain to get the price down.

Fern House was bought by 'Doc' Bewers who, like the Culeys, had just moved to Thetford. His wife, a Froebel trained teacher, opened a small 'dame' school in a room on the first floor, that jutted out over the street. She wanted to be called 'Eeker' by her pupils and whilst patients waited downstairs on scratchy, horsehair chairs to see 'Doc', she ruled her pupils in an idiosyncratic way; making them count conkers on a string rope, teaching them to read from dog eared primers of the 'cat sat on the mat' variety.

Ben and Jessie felt sorry for 'Doc'. Like them, he was a newcomer to the town and thus rather shunned by the insular Thetfordians, as he tried to garner patients. So they signed up to become first on his list.

51, Croxton Road was a semi-detached late Victorian house, very different from the spacious houses Ben had been used to. The pokey front room was flanked by a long dark hall leading to the kitchen. The small garden had a fish pond and the railway line ran alongside.

Each morning the prestigious 'York and Doncaster' express train, with its cream and brown livery, would speed by in a sweep of steam and the clatter of wheels on metal.

After I was born in 1936 it would become a daily ritual to be held up by 'Auntie Gertie', our household help, to watch it thundering past. What speed, what power!

Just down the road lived Miss Reynolds, whom I called 'Aunty Wence' because I couldn't manage her name. Neither could I manage the hard spicy taste of the ginger biscuit she would offer me and so I would 'accidentally' drop it on the linoleum floor.

Chapter Sixteen

Crazy for Cinema
The Palace – Thetford

"Cinema began with a passionate physical relationship between celluloid, craftsmen, technicians and artists, who came to know cinema as a lover knows his beloved. No matter what direction cinema takes, we cannot lose sight of its beginnings."
- Martin Scorsese

'The People's Picture Palace' was too much of a mouthful for the modest building Ben had bought from George Brown.

He simplified it to 'The Palace' and when it was re-opened in 1931 it was a 385 seat cinema.

Ben gave a free show to his first customers. On the bill was the first 'talkie' film to be shown in Thetford. It was called 'A Warm Corner' and starred Leslie Henson. An apt title, as the wooden structure suffered a further fire, which gave Ben the opportunity to take down the whole building and construct a robust, brick cinema.

The new Palace Cinema, 1931

He learnt that two large chimneys at Burrell's Engine Works and at Nickerson's Wood Yard were about to be demolished, so off he went to negotiate. If he could get the bricks for nothing it would save him buying new ones.

"If I get your chimneys down, no cost to you, can I keep the bricks?" said the cheeky young man.

It seemed like a good arrangement to the owners, although Jessie was worried sick.

"Was he going to do the job himself? He'd never attempted anything like this."

Ben however always enjoyed a challenge.

Jessie couldn't bear to watch, as with no safety harness he shinned to the top of the first chimney.

Whilst he sat up on high, knocking away each layer of bricks, along came Hilda Leech, whose husband Horace had a shop nearby.

"Hello there," she called, "That looks like hard work. Would you like a cup of tea?"

Ben shouted down,

"Yes please, Mrs Leech, just as soon as I've got this here chimney down."

That encounter led to a lifelong friendship between the Leeches and the Culeys.

Ben then worked hard to promote his business. Every week he and Jessie drove around the local villages putting 'flyers' through letter boxes, to advertise the coming week's films.

He also had the idea of using his 16 mm cine camera to photograph local events; football matches, sports days, village fetes. Then he'd show the results at the Palace and the people who'd been filmed would come along to the cinema to see themselves on the big screen.

Years later the University of East Anglia made a film including some of Ben's footage. It was called 'Ben Culey's Thetford' and sold well all over Norfolk. He was interviewed by Thetford's historian, David Osborne.

I tried to get some financial acknowledgement from the UEA film archive to help my Dad in his impoverished old age. The University of East Anglia sent him the sum of £40 as an 'honorarium'.

In the 1930s 'going to the pictures' meant the customers got full value for their money, as the programme lasted for a whole evening.

The programme changed twice a week. Monday to Wednesday then Thursday through Saturday. There were no shows on Sunday.

An evening's show consisted of two films. First would come the 'supporting' B film which might be a nature film, a travelogue or an inferior rating of film, known as a 'B' film. It was a joke that Ronald Reagan, later to become President of the United States, was only ever an actor in 'B' movies.

The first part of the programme would be followed by the Pathé newsreel, which was the only means, except for the radio, that an audience could follow world events; see their political leaders or the celebrities of those times, who were usually film stars.

Then came an interval of about twenty minutes, during which ice cream, cigarettes and soft drinks would be sold by the usherettes. Ben made sure the cinema was nice and warm, so that his patrons would need a cool drink or ice cream, for the sale of refreshments greatly enhanced the takings.

Ben had the sense to install his own electric generator, so that if there was a power cut to the general supply the show could continue. He knew that if the electricity failed the customers would demand a refund of their tickets. In this way the cinema show always went on.

It was Ben's proud boast;

"In thirty three years we only failed to put on a show ONCE and that was because the films weren't delivered on time!"

After the interval the main feature would be shown. This was the 'A' film.

At the end of the show there would be a sudden rush for the exits before the National Anthem was played over the loud speakers. Of course the more correct, civically minded citizens stood to attention for "God Save the King" before they headed for home.

Small cinemas were hampered in showing the latest films because of the hold that the large cinema circuits, such as the Odeon and ABC, had over distributors. Newly released films were firstly available in their cinemas, meaning that Thetfordians would often take the bus or train into Bury St Edmunds, so that they could boast about being the first to see the latest film; for going to the cinema, or the pub, was the main source of entertainment for most working people.

Ben found early on that film companies could demand 70 per cent of the gross takings for a block buster, such as 'The Sound of Music' in later days and up to 50 per cent for any film of merit.

Ben had the idea to introduce double seats priced 2/6d at the back of the cinema.

Courting couples didn't have much privacy for courting. Living in tightly packed houses, there were always other family members about and the winter months were too cold for evening walks. Few families could afford a car that a young fellow might borrow and at some stage of an evening snuggle up to his sweetheart. The cinema allowed a couple the chance to canoodle in the dark. As romance blossomed on the screen it blossomed off screen too. The usherettes would monitor the young couples' behaviour by flashing their torches along the rows of double seats.

Films were viewed through the blue haze of cigarette smoke, for in those far off days nearly everyone smoked as a leisure activity.

The projectionists could always tell if 'The Boss' was in the house because the beam from the projector would shine on his bald head.

Jessie would often set off through the twilight town, from Croxton Road to Guildhall Street, to be company for Ben when he had put the cinema 'to bed' and was ready to walk home late at night.

She could find her way through habit up the aisle of the darkened auditorium to Ben's usual seat and give him a friendly tweak of the nose.

One night she had arrived during a particularly shadowy moment in a film. It was so pitch black, she didn't notice that someone else was sitting in Ben's usual seat. A strange man yelped "Ouch" as the familiar tweak was given.

Jessie jumped back in horror,

"Oh, I'm so sorry. I thought you were my husband."

The other customers were getting annoyed,

"Get out of the way" they grumbled, "We can't see the screen"

Jessie slunk out. She was very embarrassed and stopped tweaking Ben's nose as a joke after that experience.

Within a year of buying the cinema Ben was able to repay the loan to his father and Mr Adams. The business became his own. He had an admirable cashier in the redoubtable Ada Clarke, who suffered no nonsense from clients and kept accounts strictly. She was a tall, austere lady who could not only bring order to an unruly queue with one frosty look but would firmly state,

"Sorry, you can't come in. I know you're prepared to pay but you've obviously had too much to drink. I can smell it; so no, I can't admit you" to customers who tried to wangle their way in. She acted as Ben's secretary and her domain was the low ceilinged office above the foyer where she presided over bagging up 'the takings' before Ben took them to the bank, chiding him,

"Now really, Mr Culey. You can't take out money from the petty cash when I've accounted for it!"

She sorted out the chaos in the office, which was piled high with cracked gramophone records, old posters of films and rolls of tickets. 'Miss Clarke' was unbending towards children, so it was a surprise to my mother when she announced

"I'm going to marry Sam Walton and I'd like Anne and her cousin to be my bridesmaids".

We wore rustling white taffeta dresses and taffeta bonnets which were so scratchy we took them off at the first opportunity. The couple were hardly able to enjoy married life together for Sam was sent to the front and was killed in active combat not long after. Some time later, Ada married again and moved to Barley in Hertfordshire.

Freda Howard, who took on the role as cashier when Ada had a night off, then became full time cashier.

Freda had a cheerful, outgoing nature. She lived with her mother in Castle Street, near the Albion pub. The influence of Hollywood was evident in Freda's choice of names for her three daughters; Norma, after Norma Shearer, Claudette, after Claudette Colbert and was the third called Paulette, after Paulette Goddard. ? This family of females lavished affection on the pig they kept in their yard. Many people turned to rearing a pig during the war years, as the government encouraged self sufficiency and 'allowed' the killing of one pig, per year, per household, to supplement the meagre meat ration.

As for the usherettes, I remember Gertie Muteham, Elsie Fisher, mother of Brian, Edie and Mrs Fayers; but there were many more.

David Prigg wrote on 'Down Memory Lane':
"My dear Mum was an usherette in the late 1940s. One night Dad swanned into the cinema and swept her off her feet. They were married for sixty two years, so I'm indebted to Mr Culey."

I wonder how many more courtships began in that little cinema and ended in marriage? Probably a lot; although there must have been some encounters that weren't as fortunate and didn't have the 'happy ending' beloved of screen writers.

The Palace's projectionist was Nelson Fayers, in charge of the pokey little room reached by an outside metal staircase. The big projector was a Kayley. The reels had to be changed over at just the right time to prevent 'jumps' in the film. It was hot and noisy in the projection room; the only bonus being that the assistant projectionist got to peep at the courting couples and spy on who was sitting with whom. Nelson lived just across the road in Pike Lane, until he married.

Later, Brian Fisher trained as a projectionist. Brian was truly in love with cinema. His favourite film was 'Cinema Paradiso,' an Italian film about life in a small Sicilian town which revolved around the cinema, not unlike the Palace in Thetford.

Neville Lockwood was taken on as a trainee projectionist and became Brian's best friend. Neville publicly declared in 'Down Memory Lane', with its memories of Thetford past that;

"Ben Culey was the best boss I ever had. He was a lovely man."

A real compliment from someone who had 'flown the coop' of a small provincial cinema; who became a projectionist in big London cinemas and had travelled widely in the cinema business.

Chapter Seventeen

Crazy for Cinema
The Avenue – Brandon

The cinema in Brandon was set back from the Newmarket Road behind a pleasant avenue of pollarded lime trees. It was owned by Stanley Lingwood, who had been badly injured in the Great War of 1914 to 1918. Stanley lived next door to the cinema in Avenue House. By 1933 his poor health was causing real concern and the cinema too was becoming run down and dilapidated. The patrons no longer enjoyed coming to his old cinema.

He knew young Ben Culey was looking for another cinema to buy and telephoned him.

"Are you financially secure enough to buy another cinema?"

After a lengthy conversation, Stanley decided,

'Right, Mr Culey, I'm ready to sell, if you're ready to buy!'

A deal was done and curiously, once again, the old timber building just happened to burn down, soon after the contract was signed.

A Bury builder, Fred Banks, was contracted to do the work on this occasion. Fred later became Mayor of Bury St Edmunds.

The Avenue Cinema, Brandon

Fred, Ben and one labourer built the 512 seater Avenue Cinema in ten weeks, from start to finish. Built from scratch to Ben's design, it was of

101

sounder construction and a more pleasing design than the Palace. It even had a gallery.

The reason for the haste was that the Bostock family of Ipswich, who ran an extensive circuit of 30 cinemas in East Anglia were keen to build cinemas in Brandon and Thetford, for cinemas were seen as the hot business of the future. Major Bostock had already taken action in Thetford by putting up scaffolding, unloading bricks and erecting a large sign, saying 'New Regal Cinema to be built here soon'.

He then tried the device of offering Ben the position of Manager at his new Brandon cinema. Major Bostock said that Ben could also have a 25% stake in the business as a shareholder, with the proviso that he would be on duty every night, and wear an evening dress suit; all for the sum of £4 a week! He didn't know the man he was dealing with!

Now, Ben was still extremely worried by this ploy, because he felt like David facing Goliath. Bostock had the advantage of a much bigger company behind him.

As always he recounted the details to Jessie, who'd been worried enough about the likelihood of another cinema in Thetford, let alone one coming to Brandon.

She got up from her sewing and hugged the worried Ben.

"The cheek of the man. There won't be enough business in Thetford or Brandon for two cinemas."

"I know that but what can I do?"

Ben determined to find out more about this Major Bostock from those who knew him and he made an interesting discovery. The war hero, Major Bostock, had an unexpected flaw that could be used to Ben's advantage.

In the morning the phone rang again.

"Major Bostock here. Come over and see me, Culey. This afternoon. At the Playhouse in Bury." he barked.

Now Ben had found out that Major Bostock, for all his business prowess was a highly superstitious man, particularly with regard to the colour green. He would refuse to do business with anyone wearing it, for he believed that green would bring bad luck to any new venture.

When Ben motored over to the Playhouse Cinema in Bury St Edmunds he felt nervous but also curious as to what might happen.

He was ushered into the great man's office sporting his best green Norfolk jacket with a green silk handkerchief he'd bought from Hansards in Thetford, just before he set off for Bury. This magnificent handkerchief was spilling out from the jacket's top pocket.

When Ben described the encounter to Jessie afterwards, he smiled mischievously.

"Bostock's face went dead white as he looked up at what appeared to be an Irishman entering his den."

Major Bostock indeed gazed in horror, as young Ben Culey now took full advantage of the situation and confronted him angrily.

"Why the hell do you want to build a cinema in Thetford, or in Brandon for that matter. I've only just got into the cinema business and I'm trying hard to make my way. What's your game? You're a bully!"

Major Bostock was hardly able to listen to what this angry young fellow was saying. He just wanted Ben Culey out of his office and out of his life.

Within a few days the offending sign in Thetford had been removed and the bricks and scaffolding was taken away.

Bostock decided to look for cinema sites elsewhere.

Jessie just gave a sigh of relief that Ben's ruse had worked.

The Avenue opened at 2.15 on Monday, February 11th 1935, with the showmanship Ben had shown at the Palace. He gave everyone a free show. The enterprise deserved a memorable opening after the problems Ben had faced.

It became known that those who considered themselves 'the elite' of Thetford would motor over to Brandon to see a show, rather than mingle with the 'hoi polloi' at the Palace.

The main problem for Ben was that the Cinematograph Exhibition Association decreed that new films must be released in Bury with its larger population before smaller towns could show them.

The Avenue had the latest British Thomas Houston projectors and two diesel engines were installed to supply power to the cinema.

Bill Bishop, later to become Chairman of Forest Heath Council, was one of the first projectionists and Michael Fenn started work there at fourteen years old. He recalls,

"I would cycle over from Lakenheath. It was my job to check if there were any smouldering cigarette ends lying on the floor after the show. Once I found a wallet.

'Good grief, look at all this money.' I said to my pal.

We took it straight to the Police Station."

Standards of honesty were instilled into youngsters in those days.

The Rex – Feltwell

During the war years Ben hired a hall at Feltwell and called it the 'Rex Cinema' after his Alsatian dog!

Feltwell was some distance from Brandon and as there were Army and RAF camps in the area, Ben thought it would give entertainment to the Forces as well as the local people. I am indebted to Mr Eric Pryer of Mildenhall, who sent me the following information.

"Mr Culey opened the cinema on Monday, 11th August 1941. The cost of a seat was 1/6d for adults and 9d for children. First films were 'Old Bill and sons' and then 'Argentina nights'. Charlie Carter was the projectionist and when he was called up for short term military service in 1946 his wife Doris took over for a year. Then Charlie continued until the cinema closed in May, 1964.

As at the two other cinemas, children were treated to Easter eggs and some of them delivered flyers around the village for 6d!

When the Rex closed the cinema seats and clock went to the Masonic hall in Thetford."

At each of the cinemas around Christmas time, in addition to the Saturday matinee for children, Ben would put on a free show and give every child an orange and a sixpenny bit, during the war years, or an ice cream when ice cream became available again after the war. This also helped the morale of the townspeople.

There used to be a Children's Home in Old Market Street and every single Saturday afternoon the children there were treated to a free show.

Olive Kent-Woolsey (nee Howes) told me that she was one of those children and how it brightened their lives. Later she worked as an usherette, rushing from her job at the International Stores, so that she could be there ready for the evening show.

Though my parents were innately kind in many ways, Ben could be a tough disciplinarian if trouble was brewing. He found his Alsatian dogs, Rex and later Hans, to be a great deterrent to hooligans. Sometimes tough boys would try to get in without paying, or 'kick up a shindig' during the performance. The usherettes found it difficult to keep them quiet. Then Ben would step forward.

"Shut up, you boys down there at the front!" he'd roar,

"Any more noise and I'll sling out the lot of you!"

This was the 'iron fist' approach but it was only a shake of the hand away from 'the velvet glove', as in the two following incidents.

Imagine a cold winter's night. It is raining hard. Ben is walking up to the cinema from Shrublands, which is only about three minutes away. He sees a bedraggled line of servicemen queuing to get into the cinema, their rough uniforms soaking wet, their breath rising like vapour on the night air.

He calls out in a loud voice,

"Come on in, lads! The show's on me tonight."

On another occasion, Cyril Germany told me this story.

"Mr Cooley (for that's how Norfolk people pronounced Culey) would let me in for 3d instead of 6d. He got to know that my Mum sold her weekly ration of bacon to make a bit of money, for times were hard. The woman I delivered it to always gave me 3d back, 'Because you're a well mannered boy.'"

Cyril continued,

"Once I was gazing in the fish and chip shop window, hungering after a helping of chips and knowing I couldn't afford to go in for some. Mr Culey came up and slipped me the 3d bit back that I'd spent on seeing the film. That meant I could go in and get some chips."

Chapter Eighteen

Crazy for Cinema
The Capitol – Hunstanton

Whilst 'young' Ben pursued his cinema career in Thetford, his father was also considering a move into the newly booming cinema business; having seen his son's early success. As a shrewd business man he was looking to diversify from farming. He began by building a cinema in Hunstanton, close to the sea front. . He called it 'The Capitol Cinema' and it opened on the 22nd of June 1932 with a musical film, entitled 'The Desert Song', starring Nelson Eddy. Ben had the building designed so that it could be used as a theatre, as well as a cinema; for astutely Ben realised that in the summer months the holiday makers who flocked to 'Sunny Hunny' would pay for a good night out at a show.

Noel Coward's play 'Private Lives' and a farce entitled 'Rookery Nook' were staged there when it opened in 1932.

The building was constructed of the local carrstone, a rust coloured, soft stone common to that corner of Norfolk. The building still holds the record for having the largest gable wall of carrstone in existence.

Ben Senior died in 1953 and the Capitol closed in the 1960s.

After some years in which the cinema business languished across the width and breadth of the country, the cinema/theatre was finally purchased by the Borough Council of King's Lynn and West Norfolk in 1981.

It was renamed the 'Princess Theatre' in honour of Diana, Princess of Wales. Diana was closely connected with this corner of Norfolk, having spent her childhood on the Sandringham Estate. As we know, Diana was tragically killed as the result of a car accident in Paris. She was only thirty nine years old.

The Princess Theatre continues to draw in the people of 'Sunny Hunny', weekenders, holiday makers and 'second homers', by staging shows featuring well known entertainers, broadcasters and television celebrities.

When the late Ken Dodd played there, rumour has it that the doors were locked so that no one could leave, as his show could go on until one in the morning!

Chapter Nineteen

Precious Cargo

It is 1935 and Ben and Jessie are still childless. Ben may have been busy building up the cinema business but surely they should have managed to conceive a child by now? They have been married for five years.

Intimate details were not discussed openly in those days, so we cannot know if there was a problem. We can only surmise that their parents must have eagerly awaited their first grand child, as Bennie was married in 1930 and Johnny in1934.

Despite some disappointment that still no baby was coming, Ben and Jessie were involving themselves in the community life of a smaller town and were getting to know people, though they often remarked,

"In Norfolk you're regarded as an outsider until you've lived twenty years in a town".

Ben's ideas of getting involved in the life of the town developed from a growing sense of civic duty. People had asked him,

"Why don't you stand for the Council? You've got plenty of ideas. Go on, shake up the Old Guard a bit."

So Ben put his name forward to become a councillor; but not as a candidate for the two main parties, Conservative or Labour; instead as an Independent, for he believed that in local politics, party allegiance was a hindrance to good decision making. Despite his inexperience in local government he topped the poll at his first attempt, even though he was a candidate with no party back up. He continued to top the polls through forty years of Council service and was very proud to be elected as Mayor three times and to be appointed an Alderman, although the title 'Alderman,' which was an honorary one, was later abolished during a re-organisation of local government.

Ben only stood down from council work in his seventies and that was because he forgot to get his nomination papers in on time.

Every one who came to the door of Shrublands with a problem was invited in, listened to and, in the generous Culey way: if it was a hard luck story, that person would leave with some cash. This endeared Ben to people.

A Thetfordian called Molly Sparrow recounted,

"I was in the butcher's getting some chops and Mr Culey quietly leaned across the counter and muttered to the butcher,

'Put that on my bill' and then he just winked at me!"

Ben joined the Auxiliary Fire Service in the mid 1930s. Did he foresee the oncoming war?

He may have sensed trouble after he had taken a Mediterranean cruise with his parents, sister Edna, brother John and his wife Olive and other assorted hangers-on. The ship was the General Von Steuben, belonging to a German shipping line based in Hamburg. The family had had no qualms about this when they booked the cruise but once embarked they found that there were 450 Nazi 'brownshirts' on board and the Culeys were the only English party.

Ben said,

"We were told by these 'brown shirts' that all passengers and crew should muster on deck every morning and salute the red, black and white Nazi flag, the swastika. Well, we were taken back at this and we decided then and there we weren't going to".

A typical Norfolk response!

Fortunately the ship's officers were not Nazis and didn't make an issue of it and the family were allowed to continue holidaying in their own way.

Because of the stand they'd taken, Ben related how,

"The ship's band delighted in playing a medley of English music every night for our benefit, as part of the entertainment."

Though the brown shirted party members stiffly ignored them for the rest of the cruise, the family didn't let it bother them. As English citizens the Culeys deemed it sensible to keep a low profile but the zeal of the Fascists on board had stirred a sense of unease in Ben, so that he began to worry about the long term prospects for peace.

With this on his mind some good news was about to lift his mood, as his twenty eighth birthday approached. It was late September, 1935. Jessie, a smile spreading over her little face, was so excited she couldn't wait to tell him something; her words came tumbling out like a babbling brook.

"Ben... I've got a surprise for you... an early one for your birthday! I've, uh, been to see Doc Bewers and I'm uh.... at last! We, um, I'm... expecting a baby!"

Jessie's eyes were shining as she burst into tears of happiness.

Ben wanted to tell everyone straight away but the more reserved Jessie felt they should wait, even though she was safely over the critical first three months. The baby was due on March 4th and Jessie hoped 'it' would arrive on that very day, for it was her father's birthday. During her months of pregnancy King George V died, his eldest son David was proclaimed King Edward VIII and then abdicated because he wanted to marry the divorcee, Wallis Simpson. The second in line to the throne, the stammering Duke of York, 'Bertie' to his family, was proclaimed King George VI.

Whilst all this was happening in the higher reaches of society, modest Jessie was preparing the layette for her baby, eagerly assisted by her mother, sisters and the Culeys in Lynn.

On 27th February 1936, Jessie walked through the quiet streets to see the new Alfred Hitchcock film, 'The Thirty Nine Steps' adapted from the novel by John Buchan, with Robert Donat in the leading role; a story of spying that was almost a premonition of the war to come.

Suddenly, as Jessie sat in the warm darkness of 'the Palace', she felt deep stomach pains gripping her, then receding. She'd been told by the nurse that this might happen when she went into labour. She wasn't frightened, she was glad that her baby was coming.

She squeezed Ben's arm as he sat beside her and whispered urgently,

"Ben, I think my time has come, a bit early. I need to get my things and go to the Nursing Home".

Ben panicked a little.

"Are you sure? Isn't it just the suspense causing your stomach to turn over?"

The film was a thriller and in Ben's mind, quite likely to cause a nervous reaction, but Jessie was adamant.

"No Ben, Ouch... It's really happening"

Ben knew then she was in real pain. Quickly he set things in order with Ada Clarke, the cashier, fetched the car and left Jessie in the care of the Nursing Home in King Street.

Soon he would be holding his son.

"Why he'll be just like me. Impatient to get on with life."

He chuckled, as he drove home to 'Lyndhurst' in Croxton Road, after making sure the cinema was locked up for the night.

"The boy wants to meet the world head on!" he thought.

Then Ben went to bed and slept soundly.

Jessie was aware of a nurse looking down at her, as she came round in a very woozy state from the chloroform. The nurse handed her a little bundle, swathed in the new cream shawl that her mother in law, Grace, had bought for the baby.

"You've got a baby daughter, Mrs Culey."

Jessie looked down at the wrinkled little face and her tears fell onto the baby's Viyella nightie. How glad she was to hold the precious baby in her arms. How relieved the ordeal was over. She wasn't very good at dealing with pain. It had been a long labour. At thirty she was considered 'old' to be a first time mother and during the 1930s the practice was that women should not push during labour, as this was supposed to cause prolapse of the womb. Holding back the natural impulse to push, during the third stage of labour, weakened her muscles and actually brought about a prolapse. For years Jessie suffered the indignity, of a dropped uterus, not feeling that she could seek medical help. I have often wondered why I didn't have brothers or sisters. I know my father wanted a son. Just as Jessie had playfully tweaked his nose in the cinema, Ben's nose was put out of joint by the fact that men he respected in Thetford had all fathered boys... but his baby was a girl and not a son.

Throughout my childhood he encouraged me to be tough, as if he could will me into becoming a tom boy and so more like the son he never had.

After the birth Jessie stayed in the nursing home for a month's bed rest. This was prescribed for mothers that could afford it. At that time it was feared that new mothers might suffer haemorrhage and puerperal fever if they weren't careful and didn't rest. Mothers who were poor wouldn't have found the time or been able to afford the luxury of bed rest. As it turned out the advice did nothing to strengthen Jessie's weakened muscles, though it enabled her to forge a lasting friendship with Mrs Mabel Hubbard, whose daughter Dorothy, born on March 4th, also became her daughter's friend.

Daddy wanted to call me Barbara but he gave way to Jessie's preference and I was christened Anne Bridget at St Nicholas Chapel in Lynn, when I was six weeks old. Being saddled with the initials A B C may have influenced my future as a teacher?

It was typical of Ben and his urge to travel, that I was but three months old when my Daddy and Granddad sailed on the second voyage of the new 'Queen Mary,' newly launched by the Cunard Line. She received a Blue Riband welcome in New York. .

Keen tourists, they visited the new Chrysler building, the Empire State building, Radio City which symbolised the USA's optimism and 'go getting' approach to the modern world, which both Bens greatly admired.

Ben Culey, father and son in New York, 1936

Whilst they enjoyed themselves in the 'Big Apple', Jessie was left 'holding the baby' and looking after the cinemas.

As I grew into a toddler two things became apparent. Mummy had worried that her little daughter would inherit the alopecia that afflicted both her father and herself. She was conscious of her thinning hair and when she became menopausal she lost all her hair and had to wear a hairpiece.

Unkindly, some women in Thetford would comment,

"Your hair looks nice, Jessie. What hairdresser do you go to?" which caused her great embarrassment.

Every night when she was expecting me Mummy would pray,

"Please God, grant my child a good head of hair" and He did.

Anne and Ben in the garden at Lyndhurst, Croxton Road.

Unfortunately Mummy neglected to pray for good eyesight and so a recessive gene in her branch of the family meant that my cousin, Bridget and I both developed a 'squint' or 'turn' in the eye.

When I was three years old I was taken to an opthamologist in Wigmore Street, London. The kind lady looked me straight in the eye and said,

"Anne's eyes are the colour of a Persian kitten's."

It was all very well to start with a compliment but then she told my parents that I had very little vision in my left eye and would need to wear glasses, with a red lens in the right eye, which would strengthen my left eye by making me use it more.

The squint was remedied by weekly sessions with the optician, Mr Large, at Bromhalls the Chemists, later to be renamed Parry and Large.

In his dark little consulting room he showed me two cards of a parrot and a cage and my 'lazy' eye had to focus on putting the parrot in the cage. Although it worked in straightening and strengthening the left eye, I've never had good vision in that eye and wearing glasses from the age of three meant that rude boys shouted "Four eyes" at me in the street.

Despite the diagnosis of their daughter's poor eyesight, life was good for Ben and Jessie. The Thetford and Brandon cinemas were doing well, the worries of the recession were past. However there were still niggles in Ben's mind about what that "Odd little Austrian with the lick of hair and funny moustache "might be up to. Strange how Britons always seem to make jokes about the things they fear.

Ben was amused by seeing Thetford boys, who'd watched Adolf Hitler on newsreels at his cinema, then strutting about the streets with stiff legs in a parody of the goose step, fingers stuck across their top lips in imitation of that strange moustache. It was a bit of fun but Ben, like other men of his age knew that the threat of Hitler was real. Still, it is curious, that in the growing crisis Ben's reaction was typically optimistic. Business was booming at the cinemas so he decided to buy a bigger house for Jessie and his daughter.

Chapter Twenty

Crazy for Cinema
The Pilot – King's Lynn

Whilst Ben and Jessie are getting used to being parents Ben senior suddenly had the right opportunity to build a cinema in King's Lynn when, sadly, his wife Grace's brother, John Chase died in June, 1938. He owned 'Garden House' in Pilot Street. The house had formerly been the 'Dog and Duck' pub. Providentially it had a large orchard, so there was enough ground for a cinema and a car park to be built in the North End and right near the town centre too. John Chase had bought the pub and land for £520 in 1914 and in 1938 it is recorded that Grace Culey bought it from his immediate family for £685. In 24 years the value of the land had only increased by £24, at £1 a year. Was the price Ben paid due to Grace being 'family' or the effects of the 1930s Depression?

John Chase, the grandson of the owner, John Chase told me,

"My Uncle Ben, telephoned Keeble Allflatt, the son of Mr Allflatt, who had built the Palace Cinema, on a Saturday morning. He said he wanted designs for his new cinema drawn up and on the table by Monday morning. Blow me, Keeble set about it and had the plans all ready on the Monday. Would that happen today?"

Not only were the plans quickly forthcoming but building work began in August and the cinema was completed in fourteen weeks. Was Ben senior showing his son that he couldn't beat him on timing? There were always elements of competition between father and son.

In his plans Ben wanted a brand new alternative cinema. He had to compete for business with the Majestic Cinema, the Theatre Royal and the old St James cinema. So he commissioned a bold Art Deco design, striking in its stark, geometric symmetry.

The foyer of The Pilot Cinema was designed to convey the ambience of an ocean liner, in keeping with the cinema's proximity to the fishing fleet and the sea going traditions of King's Lynn. Fish there were too; exotic, tropical ones, in two aquariums built into the stylish chrome decor of the foyer.

In the auditorium were wide, top quality plush seats with a geometric jazz pattern and a sweeping gallery above. It could accommodate 797 patrons and it had a staff of nine. As the customers queued for ice cream they passed statues of Egyptian slave girls standing with lamps aloft, in alcoves along the sides of the auditorium.

The focal point for the audience were the silk curtains featuring a bright galleon in full sail, which billowed realistically as the curtains opened or swirled smoothly together at the end of a show. The design was based on a tile still displayed in a museum at Coalbrookdale, Shropshire.

Ben had double seats for couples installed in the gallery, following his son's initiative at Thetford. The older, more conservative townspeople were not well pleased and instructed their daughters and the young men courting them NOT to sit there. When the lights went down there was a hurried migration amongst the courting couples to the double seats at the back. A similar rapid return to the single seats took place before the lights went up at the end of a show!

The Pilot was a much larger, grander design than the smaller Palace Cinema and it befitted the larger town.

For the Grand Opening four usherettes in smart uniforms stand on the steps with the Commissioner who is resplendent in a grand uniform with three stripes on his sleeves. Johnny Culey stands behind. He was to be Manager of the cinema.

Stephen Worfolk's book on 'The Cinema in Lynn' describes my grandfather, Ben Culey so well at this stage of his life, I must include it here;

"Mr Culey, a man of many interests, owner of fishing smacks and farms, was a colourful personality, well known in the North End; readily identified by his powerful build, visibly distressed suits and ancient trilby hat. His habit of smoking good cigars in his pipe, in which they stood like chimneys, gave him an air of imminent combustion".

The comment about suits shows the reader that Ben didn't much care how he looked. He wasn't a vain man, concerned about his appearance and the cigar in a pipe well describes the idiosyncrasy of the man's character. In other words "Take me as I am".

When Bill, his chauffeur, shaved him in the morning, Ben would rummage around in the drawer next to his armchair and try out several sets of false teeth for comfort. In exasperation he would usually throw them back in the drawer and slam it.

"None of 'em fit right" he'd grumble and generally go toothless through the day.

As Ben went about the town he invited all and sundry to a free show on the opening night of his brand new cinema.

He knew that if they were given a good time they'd come again.

Altogether 'The Pilot' had a staff of four usherettes in uniform, a doorman or commissionaire, a projectionist and an assistant, a cashier and Johnny Culey, the manager.

The New Pilot Cinema - King's Lynn

The Proprietor
requests the pleasure of the Company of

....

to the Opening
by His Worship the Mayor
(Col. Ald. G. G. Woodwark, C.B.E., T.D., J.P.)
on Monday, November 28th, at 2.15 p.m.
IF UNABLE TO ATTEND PLEASE RETURN CARD
AT YOUR EARLIEST CONVENIENCE

On Monday, 28th November1938, the commissionaire swings open the plate glass doors and nigh on eight hundred people jostle one another excitedly as they climb the steps and enter the luxurious foyer, feeling the warmth of central heating on their faces.

The new Walt Disney film, "Snow White and the Seven Dwarves" was the main feature.

During the showing of the film few of the guests knew that a little girl, only two and a half years old, was hiding under a seat in the stalls, terrified by the wicked step mother who transformed into an evil witch.

No doubt it was the first film I'd ever seen and it was hugely magnified by my closeness to the large screen. Later the witch scenes were cut from the film as being 'unsuitable for young children' but the black figure continued to haunt me in nightmares for years to come.

When the lights went up my Daddy, Ben Culey junior, took me by the hand,

"Come along Anne, we have to go on stage"

I pulled back, wishing that I could hide under the seat again. Even though I was delighted to be wearing a new pink net party dress, with ballet shoes to match, I was overwhelmed by the hugeness of the auditorium, the people, the music.

Little Anne Culey presents a bouquet to the Mayoress at the opening of the Pilot
Ben and Johnny Culey stand behind

The spotlights were so bright on my face I could hardly see. Someone came from behind the curtains at the back of the stage and thrust a huge bouquet into my clammy hands.

"Give it to that lady in the hat" she hissed.

There was a man wearing a long gold chain and a lady in a fur collared coat and hat, so I thrust the flowers towards her and she took me by the hand and said,

"Thank you, little one."

Then there was a rush of clapping that sounded like thunder.

I thought I would w-w-wet my knickers, I was so scared by it all.

Before the audience left each lady was given a box of chocolates and each man received an ounce of tobacco or a packet of cigarettes.

At Christmas time, the Mayor and Mayoress of Lynn, Councillor and Mrs CG Woodwark; for they had been the dignitaries at the opening; sent a box addressed to 'Anne Culey' to Folly House. On top of an iced cake were little figures of Snow White and the Seven Dwarves. What a kind thought. I kept the little figures for years. They regularly appeared on my birthday cakes.

'Old' Ben was fifty nine years old at the opening of the Pilot. For a shilling people could walk the short distance from cramped living quarters into the warmth of his cinema. For many it was not just entertainment but an education. Before television it was the only way they could see moving pictures of world events, politicians, other people in the news and far off lands they might never travel to.

Ben had provided dressing rooms at the back of the stage and during the war years from 1939 to 1945 he put on top class variety shows to boost people's morale. Artists that came to Lynn included George Formby (with his ukelele). He had a toothy grin used the catch phrase,

"Turned out nice again" which Ben added enthusiastically to his repertoire of imitations.

Another artist that Ben hired was Cyril Fletcher, the comedian, with big popping eyes; Jessie Matthews, a singer; Doris and Elsie Waters, who had a radio show; and their brother, Jack Warner, who starred in the film, 'The Blue Lamp' and later 'Dixon of Dock Green' on television.

There was also Hughie Green and Sandy Powell, whose catch phrase was,

"Can you hear me Mother?"

They all passed through the portals of Folly House and were generously entertained there. Sometimes they were billeted with Jessie Ireson, Grace's niece, at her home called 'Woollamalloo' after a district of Sydney, Australia.

Imbued with the spirit of all this showmanship it was small wonder that Ben and Grace's only grand daughter would find herself drawn towards play acting, when she was around the age of six. On a Saturday night I would dress up and, making an entrance from behind the red velour curtains drawn across the French windows, I would reveal myself in character as 'Mrs Faithful' or 'Mrs Courageous'. On one occasion I went too far, appearing as 'Mrs Comfortable' with not a stitch on.

The surprised adults didn't know whether they should laugh or be shocked and I saw a mixture of both emotions crossing their surprised faces.

Mummy quickly stepped forward and briskly said.

"Anne, it's time for bed."

And that was the end of it.

Chapter Twenty One

The House by the River

During the 1840s the Burrell family, whose engineering works were in St Nicholas Street, Thetford, had built their son a house called 'the Shrubberies" in Nether Row. It had gardens stretching down to the River Thet, which mingled with the waters of the Little Ouse at the weir, across from their land.

A century later when Ben was searching for a bigger home for his family, he saw a square, neglected building, choked by Virginia creepers. At the time the housing market was depressed, particularly so with the threat of an imminent war.

"Do you think we ought to be buying such a large house, if war is coming?' was Jessies's worried reaction but no one else was interested in the gloomy house, so Ben knew it was the right time to buy it.

He gave full vent to his earlier hopes of becoming an engineer by designing the house he re-named 'Shrublands'. Once again he showed loyalty to the man who'd assisted him earlier with the cinema and asked Mr Allflatt, the builder from Lynn, to undertake the renovation. With his beloved Hollywood in mind Ben wanted to transform the house into an Art Deco model, lightening and brightening the old building.

'Shrublands', the transformation underway

First he cleared away the overbearing creepers. He put in typical 1930s curved bay windows facing the river, covered the roof with Dutch green tiles, similar to the ones his father had used for Folly House and covered the red brick walls with cream plaster. The colour theme continued in the kitchen and the units in cream and green, ordered from Harrods, are still there eighty years later.

Ben installed a large American refrigerator and an electric washing machine in the re vamped kitchen, in addition to an Aga stove.

The lounge and the dining room faced each other across a spacious hall. Ben chose marble fireplaces for each room, even though he installed radiators throughout the house, powered by a massive boiler in the basement.

The dining room had a very elegant walnut cocktail cabinet in the corner, filled with crystal decanters and glasses. The unit was another purchase from Harrods.

Ben and Jessie didn't drink alcohol, except on special occasions but liked to offer drinks to their guests and the film travellers who visited to promote film hire. Cigarettes or cigars were offered from a handsome box on top of the coffee table and lit from an onyx lighter. Ben didn't smoke and Jessie would just occasionally take gentle puffs on a Balkan Sobranie cigarette at social events.

Two bathrooms were installed in the Art Deco style. One was turquoise green and one was in shiny black. There were also separate toilets on the first and ground floor. Two large bedrooms faced the river, with a box room in between, which became Anne's little bedroom.

There was a further bedroom facing Nether Row and another room downstairs for guests.

The long billiards room was reached through the kitchen and Ben converted this into a music room, complete with a Steinway grand piano that had a pianola built into it. He loved to amaze guests by his apparently skilful playing. He would sit at the key board, his hands hidden by the raised piano lid, apparently performing Liszt's Hungarian Rhapsody effortlessly, whilst the piano roll actually executed the piece.

A large conservatory fronted the music and the dining rooms and here the gardener, Bill Rudland grew exotic palms and the curly topped chrysanthemums for which he was famous.

The stairs were enhanced by a stained glass window depicting a galleon in full sail; probably the same design as the wonderful billowing sailing ship on the curtains of the Pilot cinema in Lynn. The stairs curved gracefully with shallow treads; one could imagine a Hollywood star stepping sinuously down them in a satin ball gown.

For a child the stairs were ideal, for either sliding down the smooth curving rail or tobogganing full tilt on a tray from the local Pulp Works. On the side of the house facing towards the town, Ben started to build a flat for domestic staff but because of the threat of war this was never finished.

The garden sloped down to the river and a large plane tree stood as a focal point for the garden.

The curved covered terrace leading to the garden had smooth reddish tiles and the same tiles were used on the paths leading down to the river. Half way down Ben introduced an ornate Italian fountain that splashed water into a pool below.

Soon a swing was suspended from one of the plane tree's branches and a small circular garden house, with two gothic windows, became the little play house where Anne held tea parties for her dolls.

Shrublands' garden in winter time

To the left side of the house were two large fish ponds and rockeries, flanked by vegetable beds, where asparagus made a yearly appearance.

125

Jessie loved flowers and had a great gift for flower arrangements. Fortunately the garden beds were filled with flowers from spring to autumn, so Jessie had plenty of material for her talents.

Ben, Jessie and three year old Anne moved into 'Shrublands' during July 1939.

The little family, plus faithful 'Aunt Gertie', who became the daily help, had no idea that their new home would so quickly be invaded by a great assortment of others.

The family were still adjusting to their new surroundings when six weeks later war was declared on September 3rd, 1939, bringing even greater changes to their lives.

Shrublands

Chapter Twenty Two

WAR!

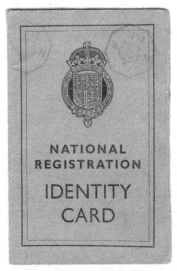

On a sunny Sunday morning, September 3rd, 1939, the people of the British Isles were informed by the Prime Minister, Neville Chamberlain, that the worst had happened. A reluctant government had finally declared war on Nazi Germany.

"Well that's it Jessie girl. The balloon's gone up, good and proper".

What did Daddy mean? I'd seen the huge silver air balloons floating above Norwich when we drove in to the city to do some shopping. They looked so pretty, shining in the sunlight. Had they got loose? Had the ropes holding them fast to the ground given way? My parents were looking so serious I didn't dare put my questions to them.

Immediately a wailing began. Daddy said the air raid warning system was being tested. I'd heard this noise before, as it alerted the firemen that there was a fire somewhere.

Daddy had dug out a deep shelter next to the house. He'd shown me inside. It had a heavy iron door and steps led down to a room with bunk beds. It was cold down there, even in late summer.

"That would've withstood the shock of an atomic bomb blast" Ben boasted in later years.

Soon there were strictures about black out curtains and not showing any lights at night, for it was expected the Luftwaffe would start bombing the East coast sea ports and cities.

Air raid wardens patrolled the streets of Thetford and quickly sprung into action if they saw a light showing. They'd bang on the door or window and shout,

"Put that light out!" even it was only a faint glimmer behind a curtain. Many people made black out screens from material and affixed them to wooden frames to cover their windows at night.

Street lamps were no longer lit and road signs were taken up,

"To confuse the enemy" if Germans troops landed. 'Pill' boxes were built. The concrete structures with slits for guns still litter our countryside. What could a couple of chaps in them taking pot shots at advancing tanks or a marching army do to hinder the enemy's advance? It's also hard to understand why they were placed in such odd positions.

If cars travelled at night their headlights had special hoods fitted to dim their lights.

Patriotic posters appeared everywhere; in shops, at the doctors' and the dentists' surgeries. Even May Chase, who wore a man's cap and had a potato sack for an apron, nailed the propaganda posters to the stable door of her little greengrocer's shop in Earl Street.

"Careless talk costs lives" and "Dig for Victory" they proclaimed.

Many people dug up their flower beds to grow vegetables. Ben persuaded Jessie to give up two rose beds, so that they could plant more produce but this included asparagus beds!

Many people gave up their iron railings and gates for the war effort.

Later on in the war, as people began to feel the pinch from fewer rations; subversive slogans began to appear. "Wot no Snoek" or "Wot no fags", they grumbled.

Ration books for food and coupons for clothes were issued. Every citizen had to carry an identity card. The number of mine was drummed into me, in case I lost it. The number was TQKD143 and it became my national health number after the war.

Everyone was issued with a gas mask. Parents could buy children a Mickey Mouse one if they wished. I thought these were babyish and preferred an ordinary khaki one. In the early days of the war we had to carry them everywhere in a canvas box slung on our shoulder, as gas attacks were feared. Little babies were encased in an awkward gas free contraption over their prams when they were outdoors.

Propaganda films such as "In Which We Serve," were made to encourage pride and patriotism.

It was thought that the film 'Mrs Miniver' actively influenced the United States to join in our fight against Fascism. There really was a sense of 'togetherness' through the darkest days of the war.

Thetford, surrounded as it was by pine forests; the sandy soil being unfit for most arable crops, made ideal terrain for training military personell. Camps sprung up for Army and Air Force servicemen.

The Stanford Battle Area was used for tank manoeuvres and other battle training.

In 1941 the army commandeered a great swathe of land encompassing the small forest settlements of Buckingham Tofts, Langford, Stanford, Sturston and West Tofts.

The villagers were evicted from their homes and have never been allowed to return to live there. The area was declared 'off limits' to civilians. Parts of it were mined. It is now known as STANTA and is still used by the army.

Ironically, amidst all the disruption and restrictions, the war years turned out to be a good time to be in the cinema business.

Young men and women were uprooted from their homes the length and breadth of the country through conscription to the forces. They were lonely and cast adrift. .

So they flocked to see the latest films at the nearest cinema; enjoying a sense of identity and companionship; sitting close together in the warm snugness and familiar smokiness of the cinema, sharing a cigarette with pals, joined together by laughing through a comic film with new comrades. Such things offset the loneliness and made them forget for a little while the dreadful homesickness that being in a strange part of the country induced. The isolation of Thetford and the grey flint buildings depressed them. Lads from urban areas missed the bustle and activity of city life. Going to 'the flicks' alleviated their fears of what might happen to them when they were called to fight the enemy.

Petrol was rationed from September 23rd September 1939 but Ben's cinema business meant that he was given extra coupons for travelling.

One summer's day in June1940, I was sitting on the porch eating marmite and tomato sandwiches when Daddy came out of the house with a very sad face.

"What's up Ben?" said Mummy "You look awful."

"France has fallen" replied Daddy.

Innocently I asked,

"Where's it fallen to?" Not knowing what 'France' was or how the fall of France to the German occupying army meant that a country, just across the English Channel from us, could give Hitler a landing pad from which to launch the imminent invasion of England.

Yet whilst all these concerns were worrying adults, they were careful to protect children from war news, which was not suitable for them to hear. News on 'the wireless' or in newsreels at the cinema was heavily censored, to make the situation seem more positive than it was.

My particular fears were concerned with starting school. When I was four and a half I attended Eeker's, the little dame school run by Doc Bewers' wife in the upstairs room that jutted over Earl Street. I can remember my pale pink coat with velvet collar and breeches, trousers that did up at the ankle with tiny buttons. It was difficult for my chubby fingers to get these breeches on and off with Eeker standing impatiently beside me, so I was relieved when Mummy quickly dispensed with the wretched things and bought more practical clothes.

Soon I was allowed to walk up the hill to school on my own; meeting my friend Dorothy and a charming, elderly gentleman called Mr Venning at Doran's Corner. He would then escort us to school with a 'tap, tap, tap' of his walking cane, doff his trilby as he bid us "Good morning" at the entrance to Fern House and proceed on his morning constitutional.

No one thought anything odd about his kindness, which was simply motivated by friendliness towards two chatty little girls.

Benjamin Guiness, son of the Earl of Iveagh, was brought from Elveden Hall every morning by pony and trap, together with his sister, Henrietta. Benjamin was a handsome, fair haired boy of seven years old. One day he was coming up the stairs to the school room complaining ;

"Urgh, that toilet downstairs really stinks."

Benjamin hadn't realised that Eeker was following him up the stairs and heard every word. Because Eeker was democratic and no respecter of rank and privilege, Master Benjamin was treated to the same punishment as any other child for his rudeness. The cane was fetched and Benjamin received four strokes on his aristocratic bottom.

One afternoon I arrived home from school in a rush to tell Mummy news about my day. I slipped on some loose sand that had oozed out from the sand bags positioned outside the front door, in case of incendiary bombs. I fell against the pillar and cut my forehead.

Mummy heard my cries and ran to pick me up.

"Anne, what have you done now!" she cried. Behind her I could see an unfamiliar figure hanging back, a little uncertainly in the hall. Whilst she stemmed the blood Mummy explained,

"This is Linga, she's coming to live with us. Isn't it nice? She'll be like a big sister for you." Well, this was a surprise!

Linga Albert was billeted with us because Leytonstone Grammar School in East London had been evacuated 'en bloc' to Thetford and would merge with the Girls' Grammar School. My parents, Ben and Jessie, had been allocated two of the girls, Linga and Doris. They were fifteen years old.

Our evacuees, Doris and Linga

Doris was so homesick she went back to Leytonstone after a fortnight but Linga stayed on and considered herself lucky to have found us, as she had had an unhappy childhood. I can only remember her mother coming to visit her once. Indeed Linga regarded Mummy as her second mother, although she always insisted on addressing her formally, as 'Mrs Culey'.

When Linga was old enough she joined the WAAF and was stationed in Scotland. When she came 'home' on leave Daddy would tease her by asking pointed questions about the secret work she was doing. True to her signing of the Official Secrets Act she never let fall one word about her job, although Daddy had rightly surmised that she was working on the development of radar.

Linga in WAAF uniform, a proud Anne beside her 'sister'.

When the war ended Linga took advantage of the one year government training scheme for new teachers and emigrated to South Africa, to educate girls of the Xhosa tribe, who wanted to become teachers. She kept in touch with our family until she died in 1998.

Linga wasn't the only one who lived with us through the war years.

Our home took in an ever moving stream of people, washed up there through the changing tides of war. Captain Flood, an Army officer from Australia, and a New Zealand Air force officer, also lodged with us at different times. There was also an English airman with his wife, Mrs Griffin and daughter, Pauline, who were billeted downstairs. Pauline, the same age as me, later became a leading light in the King's Lynn Amateur Dramatic Society.

One Sunday evening we were driving home to Thetford from visiting my grand parents in Lynn. I was sitting in the back of the car with Linga. It was early summer, the days were long and the trees on each side of the road from Mundford were in full leaf. Suddenly we heard the roar of plane engines and caught sight of them flying low over the land to our right,

"They're Dorniers, heading to smash up the railway line," yelled Daddy.

Mummy shouted "Put your foot down hard Ben! Get us home as quick as you can".

I had never heard my mother tell my father what to do, let alone to 'go faster' in the car.

She twisted back and pushed my head towards the floor, urging Linga too,

"Get your heads down, as low as you can".

We saw the dark shapes of the planes fly low over the railway line and heard explosions. Our small car rocked violently.

Thank goodness we were hidden by the trees.

We reached Shrublands in record time and hurried down the steps of the air raid shelter, where the lodgers were already assembled. There was a chorus of voices.

"Oh we're glad you're home. The siren sounded ten minutes ago, so we came down here. There must have been bombs dropping, we heard the thumps."

It was the first and last time I'd ever heard Mummy directing Daddy. She was a heroine, especially as she was frightened of speed.

Next day Ben went back to search the woods because there were rumours in the town about a fifth columnist; someone who secretly supported the Nazi cause. Ben had a suspicion that the German aircraft had been guided towards the main LNER railway line by this traitor and when he found evidence of a fire and the remains of a flare he reported the matter to the police. War breeds rumours, some true, some false. At the end of the war, papers were found in a certain house, which revealed a 'hit list'. Ben Culey's name was near the top as 'dangerous to the Nazi cause' and we learnt that our house would have been requisitioned for use by German Army officers.

In September 1940 the 'Baedecker' bombing raids began. The Luftwaffe targeted England's cathedral cities as a means of smashing British morale as well as her cherished buildings.

Lying in my little bedroom, its wallpaper featuring 'Snow White and the Seven Dwarves', I learnt the difference between 'our' planes and the deep monotonous 'thrum, thrum, thrum' of the German bombers passing overhead to bomb Norwich.

The bulbous anti aircraft balloons flying in the skies above Norwich had disappeared, being deemed ineffectual as a deterrent to enemy bombers.

One night I couldn't get to sleep because of the constant hum of the planes flying overhead. I was really fearful, imagining that the pilots could look right down and see me in my little bed. Daddy came into the room.

"Anne, are you still awake? Come into the garden and look at the sky."

We found our way down stairs quietly, for Mummy was asleep. We stepped into the dark garden. But the sky wasn't dark. Over to the north west of us the heavens were lit by a deep red, pulsing glow.

"Norwich is getting it tonight" Daddy said, holding my hand tightly in his strong grasp.

Not long after that we drove over to Norwich to get Mummy a winter coat at Bonds, her favourite department store. She had enough coupons in her ration book to buy a new one. We saw another department store that had suffered a direct hit. It was a blackened ruin, nothing was left.

Fortunately Norwich Cathedral, which was the target in these raids, remained proudly intact, unlike Coventry's Cathedral, which was razed to the ground.

When we made the occasional visit to London, our route took us through the East End and here the devastation was appalling. People's homes were split in half, the plaster ceilings had fallen down; ripped wallpaper was exposed to the elements; a bath was perched precariously on the edge of a cliff, where the outside wall had been ripped off by bomb blast; broken chairs, prams and piles of debris spilled onto the road.

Nobody, however hard they tried, could protect a child's eyes from that and I wondered what had become of the people who lived there.

Chapter Twenty Three

Dig for Victory

Harvesting during the War years

Early in the war the call had gone out for more agricultural land to be put into production, so that the nation could provide food entirely on its own shores.

The sea routes had been effectively closed to imports from the Empire, due to the increasing activities of German U boats, which were patrolling our coasts and torpedoing our merchant ships.

Ben was now in a position to 'put his shoulder to the plough,' metaphorically speaking. He wanted to help in producing food for the country. Business at the cinemas was good and his cinemas were boosting the morale of the townspeople and service personnel.

He decided to rent two farms. And then he bought a third farm.

Jessie was horrified.

"I can't believe it" she said, turning pale,

"After all the heartache we suffered at Middleton. You want to go back to farming?"

The first farm Ben rented was Green Lane Farm, owned by Lord Fisher of Kilverstone.

Green Lane itself was a favourite walk for Thetfordians, Starting on Melford Common walkers passed the Keymer's cottage with Redgate Farm on the left and continued along the track as it became narrower, with trees on each side, protecting walkers from the sun.

Green Lane Farm could be glimpsed down a track to the right. The lane continued until walkers turned left onto Joe Blunt's lane at Kilverstone, returning to Thetford along the Croxton Road.

Green Lane farm was old fashioned,; a traditional, mixed farm, with two hard working Norfolk farm labourers, referred to as 'hands'. An appropriate term because the hard work on such a farm mainly involved men toiling with their hands.

Nathan and Aaron, father and son, loved and cared for the huge, gentle Shire horses, with massive shoulders and feathered fetlocks. These provided the horse power for the farm; pulling the plough, other implements and carts. But life on a farm like this, without tractors, meant back breaking toil for the men and the horses.

I remember one winter's day when Daddy and I found Nathan and Aaron huddled in a shed, staring out at the relentless rain; they looked so cold in their old rough jackets, which steamed slightly from their body heat, their noses dripping like the rain drops splashing on the corrugated iron roof, raw chapped hands, frayed sleeves, the potatoes they'd dug from the field heaped beside them. It was a wretched scene and Ben determined to make life better for the men.

So it was at this farm Ben stabled the twenty two race horses evacuated from Brickfield Stud, Exning, Newmarket. The racecourse had been turned into a temporary aerodrome and many of the stables had 'evacuated' their horses to farms in the area.

Ben was proud of the fact that one of the mares successfully produced a foal. He named her Stephanotis. Her mother was Sterope. When she was old enough Ben entered her in a race called the Cambridgeshire and she won twice. The horse's owner received the prize money but perhaps Ben put a bet on her winning?

He received 'bed and board' money for looking after these thoroughbreds.

Stephanotis and Sterope on Shrublands' lawn

One day Ben and Jessie were attending a horse sale at Tattersall's in Newmarket, where one of these racehorses was to be sold. The couple had been separated in the crowd. When Jessie saw the stocky, familiar figure on the other side of the ring she waved her handkerchief,

"Ben, Ben, I'm over here!"

The auctioneer saw the raised white handkerchief as a bid and Ben was alarmed that he would be landed with a stallion he didn't want, with a large price to pay. Fortunately the bidding continued and Ben breathed easily again.

The second acreage Ben rented was part of Lord Musker's Nunnery Estate.

Tut Hill Farm covered a thousand acres. it was mainly a large expanse of fallow land, covered with bracken and brambles, just off the road to Euston. Ben hoped it could be usefully turned into productive wheat growing land, once it had been cleared.

That took some time and effort. But by the next spring it was sown with a crop of wheat and the young corn developed well on soil which hadn't been used before. .

The wheat was ripening well, the grain swelling daily under the sun's influence.

Imagine Ben's fury when he drove up Tut Hill and found tanks ploughing through this first crop of healthy, ripening wheat. Amidst the roar of noise and the imminent destruction of the entire field of wheat, he jumped out of his truck and ran, without thought of his own safety, towards the leading tank, waving his arms furiously and shouting loudly.

Fortunately the officer commanded his men to halt their vehicles in the nick of time, or Ben would've been flattened like the corn.

"What the hell do you think you're doing?" Ben bellowed.

After a heated exchange he managed to persuade the officer to delay the tanks proceeding any further until he'd contacted their commanding officer. Then he drove at break neck speed back to Shrublands and snatched up the telephone, demanding to speak to the top man in charge of the Stanford Battle Area. He was passed from one level of security to another, until at last he put his complaint before the chief officer.

"My men are on maneouvres" The high ranking Army officer barked in response to Ben's complaint.

"Well you can juddy well tell them to manoueuvre somewhere else. Order 'em off my land sharpish. I'm producing wheat for the war effort and your tanks are rampaging through my fields and destroying the whole crop."

The tanks were withdrawn and Ben was able to claim compensation for the damage.

On another occasion tanks were sent on an exercise to 'manoeuvre' their way through Thetford's narrow streets. An acquaintance of Jessie's wasn't quick enough to move her foot as the cumbersome tank accidentally mounted the pavement. Because of the damage she had to be fitted with an artificial leg.

The hazards of war affected even a sleepy little town like Thetford.

Ben bought a third farm from Sir William Gentle for £2,500 in September, 1942, securing a mortgage for £1000. Redgate Farm, was on the left where Green Lane began, just north of Melford Common. It was a small mixed farm, composed of arable land and livestock. It was managed by Mr Ernie Page. Sadly his wife had multiple sclerosis. Their daughter Ivy, was later to marry Kenny Armes, a tall blond farm worker, son of Thetford's Station Master and brother of Colin, who became a much loved Councillor. Kenny's work mate was George Hopkins, who later married one of the Land Girls from Yorkshire. Several of these girls were billeted at the farm. There was also George Angus, a Geordie, a most reliable man.

I remember the pretty Jersey cows kept at Redgate which produced delicious full fat milk. The cream was skimmed off and left to settle in large bowls in the dairy before it was made into butter.

I would walk to Redgate Farm to collect our milk in a small metal milk churn. When Mummy had some of the cream at home she would pour it into a butter churner and then slap the butter into shape with two wooden paddles. Together with chickens and egg production, we were able to supplement the rations of our household, which now consisted of evacuees and personnel from the armed forces.

When we made the occasional visit to London Mummy and Daddy would laugh at me for preferring the hotel's reconstituted scrambled egg to real eggs from our farm.

Ben's decision to go back to farming had worked out well for the household and Jessie came round to thinking it had been a good move after all.

The government allowed us to kill one pig a year for our own use. I remember the scenes at Folly House when their pig was carved up in the kitchen. The stench of fresh blood, the sight of warm flesh, layers of fat and white bones protruding made me feel sick. Daddy didn't believe in shielding me from the realities of life. He thought he had a duty to 'toughen me up'. He would have metered out similar treatment to the son he never had.

My first experience of birth was being taken to see the baby pigs or calves arriving on the farms.

"Go on Jessie, let her come," he'd say, if Mummy protested,

"Ben, she's too young. "

"She needs to see what goes on."

This was the tough Norfolk approach. It was a bloody business, which shocked me, yet the wonder of it surmounted my initial distress. The little calves would suck my fingers and I could run my hands over their rough coats. When born they all had blue eyes and it grieved me that soon the little bulls would inevitably be taken from their mothers and sent to the slaughterhouse, or sold on to be castrated and raised as bullocks for the meat market.

After the war, always ready to try the latest trend, Ben installed battery houses on Redgate Farm and I was upset to see how the chickens were housed so tightly in wire cages and how they would pluck out their feathers in distress.

During the war Ben loved to exercise Burma, a big chestnut stallion with a will of his own. He was one of the horses that Ben looked after from Brickfield Stud.

Mr Hailes in Nether Row, holding Burma

One day we were out shopping in Castle Street and Mummy glimpsed Daddy going slowly past in a taxi. She rapped on the window.

"Ben, what on earth are you doing in there?"

Then she noticed that his right arm was strapped tight in a sling.

"I'm just going home from the 'ospital," he said. "Burma threw me. I got hold of him and managed to walk him back to Green Lane but I had to get a taxi to the 'ospital. I've juddy well broken my collar bone."

Collar bones mend but Ben had a closer shave coming.

140

It was harvest time on Tutt Hill, which meant taking advantage of the long summer evenings to get the harvest in.

Jessie grumbled, "You're working yourself too hard, Ben, what with working on the farm to get the sheaves stacked, then going on to the cinema. You should leave that to Ada Clarke and Freda, they're competent."

Ben clutched at his stomach.

"Jessie I'm knackered. Don't go on at me. I've got a right ole stitch in me side".

Days passed. Jessie would catch Ben wincing with pain at times.

"Look at you, Ben. I can't bear to see you like this. You ought to go and see Doc Bewers. That pain's been going on some time and you look kind of pale under the tan you've got from being out on the fields."

It was clear that Jess had real concerns. As the stoical daughter of William White, who eschewed doctors and medicine, except for his store of little white Arnica pills, she didn't usually advise a visit to the doctor.

Two more days passed. Harvesting couldn't wait.

On the afternoon of the third day the telephone rang and Jessie hurried through the cool hall to pick up the phone.

"Hello, Mrs Culey here. Who's calling?"

"Ah, Mrs Culey. Doc Bewers here. I've had a call about Ben. He's been rushed to Bury Hospital by ambulance."

Dr Bewers, never one to waste words, rang off.

Jessie phoned the hospital in Bury St Edmunds. Ben had had an emergency operation and was recovering in the Bristol Annexe. Hastily she packed the necessary items for his stay; pyjamas, slippers, dressing gown, a toilet bag and his bedside reading, which was a copy of 'The Farmer's Weekly'.

With shaking hands she backed the car out of the garage, made arrangements for someone to look after Anne when she returned from school and set off for Bury St Edmunds. It seemed the longest twelve miles she'd ever driven.

There were few private cars on the roads during the war years because of restrictions on petrol. Coupons fetched a high price on the Black Market. In East Anglia the traffic consisted mainly of military vehicles, army and air force trucks, sometimes tanks and armoured cars and just a few commercial vehicles, as most goods were transported by train.

A neatly dressed nurse in blue uniform and starched white headdress took her to Ben's bedside.

The wan face of Ben greeted her with a weak smile.

"Hello Sweetheart. I'm juddy lucky. The boys on Tut hill saved me. I collapsed on the tractor. One of 'em jumped up and pulled on the brake and one of 'em got on his bike and pedalled like fury all the way to the nearest phone to phone for an ambulance. He took the change outa my jacket pocket.

I was in agony. Apparently they caught the peritonitis in the nick o'time. My old appendix 's ruptured. They say in another 24 hours I'd have been dead."

Jessie sank on to the chair beside the bed and held his big strong hand in her small one. Her tears splashed onto the starched white sheet. The title of a Laurel and Hardy film title sprang to mind, "Another Fine Mess!"

Thank God, her Ben had pulled through.

The harvest was safely gathered in without 'The Boss' overseeing it and Ben emerged from the Bristol Annexe, a little shakily, just over a week later and a full stone lighter.

There was no National Health Service at that time. It was just a dream in the mind of Aneurin Bevan, a Socialist MP. All treatments and surgery had to be paid for and the Bristol Annexe was for patients prepared to pay a little more. The care Ben received there saved his life.

By co-incidence the building later became Cornwallis Court, a Masonic Retirement Home and both Jessie and Ben ended their days there.

Chapter Twenty Four

Heacham Hall

Grace and Ben had probably been more alarmed than their son Bennie at the prospect of another war, only twenty years after the 'war to end all wars'.

King's Lynn had been one of the first towns in England to suffer bombing raids in the First World War. An airship had targeted the docks in King's Lynn, instead it hit a house in the North End and killed three innocent civilians. In those days this was a new kind of atrocity. Ben and Grace lived at Folly House in Gaywood, which, though a suburb, was still near to the river and the docks.

They were anxious to move out of harm's way.

"Grace, see here. Cruso and Wilkins have sent details of a place in Heacham that might suit us."

Grace casts a wary eye over the photo.

"That look a big old place. Dew we need suffin' as big as that?"

Ben persists.

"Come yew on. Let's take a gander at it. That'd d be handy for me to keep an eye on them runnin' the cinema in Hun'ston."

Heacham Hall had originally been a Tudor mansion, home to John Rolfe, who had married the Native American princess, Pocahontas in the 17th century.

The current Heacham Hall was of later construction and the Strachan family had lived there since the early 1900s. The head of the family had recently died and so the property had been put on the market.

Granddad no doubt drove one of his bargains to get it at a reduced price.

Heacham Hall had extensive parklands and a walled garden where vegetables and plants flourished, protected by the warm russet walls of carrstone which were covered by espaliered pears and peaches that ripened early, safe from the sea winds.

One day I remember my grandma saying,

"Come and have a look at this Anne," as she led me towards a haystack on their land. She parted the straw.

"Why" I gasped "It's your little house."

This was my baby name for a caravan, for I was only three years old at the time.

I still can't fathom why they had hidden it inside a haystack to keep it secret in the event of a German invasion. A fire would have destroyed it easily.

What was the point?

Before Grace and Ben had a chance to move in, Heacham Hall was requisitioned by the War Department and they had to stay at Folly House anyway.

RAF personnel moved in. There were firm instructions that no fires should be lit in the wood panelled rooms to prevent damage to the fabric but the boys in blue found it 'bloomin' freezing in the winter months, for there was no central heating. Ciggies didn't give out enough heat to warm a chap.

One bold lad decided he'd had enough. He brought in twigs for kindling and found some old logs stacked in an outhouse.

Soon he had a small fire going in the ornate fireplace and the lads gathered round, warming their hands, faces and chilled feet before the gathering blaze.

"Good old Spud" they chortled, clapping him on the back.

Suddenly the bell rang for muster. They knew this meant an inspection. Whilst they lined up outside someone could snoop around and find out what they'd done!

Spud, the thickhead, grabbed a coal scuttle from the fire irons on the grate, shovelled the brightly burning fire into an alcove and pulled the curtain across, then raced out to join his mates on the drive.

Every chap's uniform had been scrutinized and Spud had been told off for not polishing his buttons. The inspection ended and the squad were allowed to "Stand Down".

As the men filed back into the Hall they stared dumbstruck to see blue smoke billowing out from beneath the heavy oak door of their quarters.

Whilst the lads were outside, draughts in the spacious room had fanned the flames, and the fire, growing in its appetite, had quickly eaten the bone dry fabric of the curtains, gaining strength as it demolished the furniture and voraciously tackled the wood panelling, which was dry as tinder. This was what it craved.

Too late for puny water buckets as the young men tried helplessly to douse the flames and were driven back by the heat of the blaze.

An officer hastened to the phone and dialled 999.

"Urgent. We need a fire appliance uh- two or more- Heacham Hall. Hurry it's vital" and slammed down the phone.

He barked at the hot faced, bewildered men.

"Evacuate the premises. Chop chop. No time to get your kit. Assemble in the walled garden."

Thirty miles away in Thetford a phone rings at the little school called 'Fern House. '

I am counting conkers in a desultory way, for I hate arithmetic lessons.

"Hello, Mrs Bewers. This is Mrs Culey. Sorry but I have to fetch Anne. We have to go to Lynn immediately"

This was war time, 1942. Emergencies were the order of the day. No need for questions. My teacher, the redoubtable 'Eeker,' didn't waste words.

"Anne. Get your coat on, change into your outdoor shoes and take your satchel. Mummy and Daddy will be fetching you in five minutes. Stand in the porch so that you're ready to go."

I felt relief to escape from the awful arithmetic lesson. Everyone gawped at me as I left the room.

Daddy put his foot hard down on the accelerator and we flew along the quiet roads, empty except for the occasional army truck.

We didn't go to Lynn but carried on, past Folly House towards Hunstanton.

"Are we going to the seaside?" I asked excitedly. I dimly remembered a time when the beaches weren't mined and hoped perhaps things had changed?

"No," Mummy replied. "We're going to Heacham Hall. Do you remember it? Well it's on fire."

"On fire? What, that big, big house?"

Eight fire engines were parked at all angles on the drive. Huge columns of water were shooting upwards towards the burning roof. I could see sudden tongues of red and yellow flame bursting through the plumes of dense black smoke. Even from the back seat of our car the smell of it made me cough and splutter.

Mummy and Daddy were already out of the car to look but they were shouted at by a grimy fireman,

"Stand well back. Go right back!" he yelled.

I climbed out of the car and looking back saw my granddad and grandma huddled together near the walled garden. I ran to them and they hugged me tight. Their clothes smelt of the times we had a bonfire in the garden.

Why was I fetched from school? What were my grandparents doing there? Much later I asked these questions of myself.

The family had converged on the site to see if anything could be salvaged from the blaze.

The only objects rescued from the fire consisted of; a pair of intricate wrought iron garden gates, three monogrammed wine glasses and an oil painting of Miss Strachan.

The Strachan wine goblets

What happened to Spud, who so foolishly initiated the blaze? Surely he was put on charge? Or did his friends cover for him? I know that Granddad received minimal compensation. Was the loss judged paltry amidst the many losses of the war years? Questions about the fire remain unanswered and can never be solved.

The walled garden succumbed to brambles. Nettles choked the broken skeletons of the cucumber frames and a notice on a rusting gate warned,

"Keep Out! Property of King's Lynn and West Norfolk Council."

The smoking hulk of the handsome Hall gradually cooled and the ash was scattered in the wind but the stark blackened ruin was a reproach to arsonists for many years.

The remaining buildings mouldered slowly into rubble and were razed to the ground. The name 'Hall Close,' given to a small group of houses that were finally built on the site, is the only reminder of the once splendid Heacham Hall.

Chapter Twenty Five

Hay for the Horses

Mr Hailes was a wiry little man of uncertain age. he had the weathered face and the bowed legs of many years spent riding horses. Ben had inherited him with the race horses and thought that as he had a fully qualified horseman and former jockey to hand, he might as well buy a pony for his daughter.

Mr Hailes could easily care for a pony and teach Anne to ride.

"Look Jess," he said, "Here in the 'Horse and Hound'. A nice Welsh pony, 14 hands high. The previous child who rode him has been sent to Canada for the duration."

'Duration' meant for how long the war might last.

Jessie sniffed. She didn't approve of children being sent far away from their homes, war or no war and although she didn't know much about horses, '14 hands high' seemed awfully big for a child of six to manage.

She told Ben how she felt.

"Oh, she'll grow into it, "

was Ben's airy response. He'd already made up his mind.

The pony, Peter, was duly dispatched from Broadway railway station in Worcestershire and travelled all the way to Thetford by train. The fare cost Ben £5.

He was supposed to be a quiet, well trained pony but he was frisky, had a will of his own and loved to throw me off, much to my embarrassment.

"Get up and get on, Miss Hanne," Mr Hailes commanded. "Show him who's boss". but Peter sensed I was afraid and did all he could to wield pony power over me; twisting and turning, bucking and prancing to tip me off and show that he was in charge.

There was such a lot to remember as I tried to sit up straight, keep my knees tight against Peter's sides and direct him with a pull of the reins.

Every time I rode him the shout went up, "Keep your harms hin Miss Hanne," from Mr Hailes, as I struggled to keep Peter on a tight rein.

Mr Hailes had a wonderful knack for putting his 'h's' where they had no right to be and neglecting to put them where they should have been. This often led to Mummy and I having a fit of the giggles.

"We ain't got no 'ay for the 'orses,"

He announced as we set off for a horse show at Watton and the giggling in our car helped to allay my fears about the event.

Anne and Peter in Nether Row

I can remember the smell of the warm leather saddle whilst Peter flicks his ears and tail at the flies buzzing round us on a hot summer's day. I'm playing anxiously with the reins. Suddenly my number is called over the loud hailer. I click my tongue and Peter moves smartly forward. Mummy and Daddy are in the stand. I want to please them We gather pace as he approaches the first fence. I can smell Peter's sweat as he takes the fence easily. Phew. ! I regain my balance as we turn and head for the next jump. My heart is pounding. I feel cold with fear. This is the big one. Peter sails into the air but his back foot catches on the top rail and I fly through the air, landing in a heap on the dry scratchy grass. I've kept hold of the reins though, so I pick myself up. "What will Daddy think?" buzzes in my brain.

150

As I get my foot in the stirrup and heave my leg over the saddle my heart floods with gratitude, for some people in the stand are clapping and cheering me on.

A little girl on a big pony.

Daddy's pleased because I'm awarded second prize and I went home proudly with a blue rosette.

I was never a natural rider like my cousin Margaret, who fearlessly rode her big pony, a strawberry roan called Winston.

Ben really would have preferred a tomboy; ready to have a go at all sports, whereas I was the sort of child who always had my head in a book.

"You'll strain your eyes" was the constant reproof from Mummy and Daddy.

Ben was trying to find another means of getting around. Due to the petrol restrictions he'd been allowed to install a petrol pump in the yard of Shrublands. But the petrol allowed for 'agricultural purpose' was dyed orange, so that it couldn't be used for private motoring.

"A pony and trap'll be the answer for short journeys" he thought.

One morning as Jessie and Gertie were sorting out the washing in the kitchen, there was a knock on the window. Outside Ben was grinning at them and mouthing something like "Guess what I've got?"

Then there was a clatter of hooves and Ben led a chestnut mare into the kitchen.

"Get that great animal out of here at once!" shrieked Jessie.

"See how quiet she is" Ben said. But Jessie was adamant,

"Take her outside this minute!"

Outside the front door Ben put Peggy between the shafts of the smart trap he'd also bought and persuaded Jessie and Gertie to leave the washing and come for a ride. Once they'd squeezed into the back of the trap, Ben got up in the driver's seat and took the reins into his big strong hands. He urged Peggy forward with a click of the tongue and the mare started to move to his command; but instead of going directly forward she wanted to go in a circular direction, so Ben was pulling strongly on the reins, trying to keep her going in a forward direction.

"Maybe she needs more space, Jess" he said over his shoulder.

"Why don't you pack up a picnic and we'll go to Two Mile Bottom"

Jessie and Gertie climbed down and cobbled together a quick picnic before the party set out for a favourite place for picnics in the forest by the river.

All the way there Ben was struggling to keep Peggy moving forward. He was correcting her so strongly by pulling hard on the reins that the muscles in his arms were hurting badly by the time they arrived.

The usually cheerful Ben was very quiet during the picnic. He realized he had made a big mistake in being so ready to buy Peggy.

After asking the questions he should have thought of asking earlier, Ben found out that Peggy had been a circus horse and had only ever been used for moving patiently around a circus ring whilst bare back riders jumped on and off her strong, steady back. No wonder she still wanted to go round in circles all the time!

Needless to say Peggy was soon returned to the sales ring. Ben had learnt a lesson and the idea of getting around by horse and trap was solved by carefully choosing a little horse fit for the purpose.

Chapter Twenty Six

Fire Service Antics and 'Holidays at Home'

Ben in the AFS, 1936

In 1936 Ben had joined the Auxiliary Fire Service. It became the National Fire Service at the outbreak of war. Ben wanted to join the army but as he was only offered a post in the Royal Army Ordnance Corps, which supplied munitions and food to the troops, he thought better of it. He was in a reserved occupation anyway. Civilians had to join one of the supplementary services as part of everyone's effort to protect the nation. A former Army officer, Mr Graham Witton, was in charge of the Home Guard. It is common knowledge that the fictional television series, 'Dad's Army,' based on the Home Guard, was filmed in and around Thetford.

The Fire Service was called out to deal with domestic and factory fires and dispose of the unexploded bombs dropped by enemy planes jettisoning their load before returning to base. They also collected the dummy bombs dropped by our own bombers when they practiced hitting a target.

The Thetford Fire Service personnel outside the Fire Station in Cage Lane.

The fire service were on constant alert and firemen could be summoned at any time of the day or night. Ben used to recount a story of one particular call.

"One night I was on duty and a call came in that there was a fire at Cranworth Rectory: so we roared off in the fire engine, through the darkness of Thetford forest. There was a tree lined drive leading to the Rectory, no lights to be seen and no sign of a fire either.

"Go on Ben, you've got the nerve, go in and see what's up" Russell Snelling, the officer in charge said to me. Algy Ellis and Ben Thacker didn't envy me. But I'm up for a challenge, so I head off up the steps to the front door. It was very dark that night; no moon, no stars either, as it was cloudy.

I was about to knock but turned the door knob and to my surprise I found they'd forgotten to lock the door. 'Duzzy fools!' I thought. So I walked in, calling out,

'Hello, is anyone there?'

No answer. I felt apprehensive as I made my way up the stairs. They creaked at every tread Still there was no answer to my call. I wondered what mystery I might discover in that spooky old house. I reached the top of the stairs and my torch beam picked out another door. Again, I knocked and my heart was knocking too in my chest.

I turned the door knob and flashed my light around the room. There ahead of me in a four poster bed I could see the shape of two bodies, hidden by the covers, lying very still. Were they dead? I was scared.

"Hello" I said in a faint voice "Are you alright?"

At this a flannel night cap appeared, followed by a small white face, as white as the sheet it was clasping to it's chin. Two eyes were squinting at me in the glare of the torchlight. . I lowered the beam.

"Sorry, I couldn't find any light switches," I said.

Another head appeared. It was the Rector's wife, grey haired and pale faced. A bony hand reached out to search for spectacles on the bedside table. Then she felt for her false teeth from a tumbler,. Her head disappeared again under the sheets and popped up again, false teeth in place.

At last the terrified rector managed to speak.

"We thought the Germans had landed" he said "The noise of your fireman's boots sounded like German jack boots."

There wasn't a fire anywhere. That place was as cold as a morgue.

Was it some prankster's idea of a joke to summons the Fire Brigade on a fool's errand?

I apologised, saying we'd been given false information. Then I beat a hasty retreat down the stairs but oh, that old fellow looked a picture, shivering like a jelly, with a night cap askew on his grey head!

We headed back to Thetford, pretty put out by the waste of time and yet it made a good story afterwards!"

The public had been expressly warned about the danger of picking up any kind of bomb. How could they know the difference between an unexploded bomb or a dummy one?

Ben, always a bit of a dare devil, had assembled a collection of exploded bombs in the yard of Shrublands and he had an idea for using a one thousand pound bomb that the Fire Service had found near the Elveden War Memorial on the London Road.

It was brought back to the Guildhall and Thetfordians were encouraged to put cash in it 'to aid the War effort'. However, Ben got to hear that the authorities were shortly to pay him a visit and arrest him for 'purloining' this big bomb.

After emptying out the collected money he hastily hoisted it into his car, took it back to Shrublands and dumped it in the river without delay. And there it remains to this day.

Holidaying at home

About the time of these adventures I had my tonsils and adenoids removed by our Doctor in the Cottage hospital. It was done under anaesthetic. A rubber mask was placed over my mouth and I had to count to ten. The following night, whilst two of us recuperated on a ward, the air raid siren sounded and Charles Watson, son of the Grammar School Headmaster, and I, cowered in our beds and felt very homesick.

The compensation was that we were given marmite and tomato sandwiches and jelly to soothe our sore throats.

Shortly afterwards I developed a high temperature and Dr Bewers was called to Shrublands.

"Anne has scarlet fever," he pronounced. "She has a high temperature and an abcess in the left ear. Move her bed downstairs and keep an eye on her."

Doc Bewers was a good doctor but he didn't have a comforting bedside manner.

When he came to see me again he told my mother,

"The sea air would do her good now she's getting better but where can you go these days?"

The beaches around the East coast were mined, in anticipation of a German invasion and so 'out of bounds' but the West coast beaches of Devon had not been mined.

Anne and Jessie, Ilfracombe 1943

We travelled by train to Barnstable and handed our ration books to the hotel receptionist. It was the first time I had stayed in a hotel. By this time I was an avid reader, having progressed from the horrible dog eared 'readers' at Eeker's.

I loved the Mary Plain books by Gwynedd Rae. I would giggle out loud at the misadventures of Mary, a small brown bear. My chuckles caused some amusement amongst the guests in the hotel lounge.

Whilst we were there the newspapers announced that Italy had changed sides. Instead of being on the side of the Nazis they had decided to join 'the allies'.

I played amongst the rock pools of Croyde Bay and Coombe Martin and Daddy tied knots in the corners of his big man's handkerchief and wore it like a cap, to protect his balding head from the sun. Wartime summers always seemed to have been sunny. Is it just a trick of the memory that makes us remember the good summers when we are young?

Devon was out of reach for most people. Even short trips were out of the question for many. So every year the local council would lay on a week of entertainment and call it 'Holiday at Home'. There would be fancy dress shows, fetes, gymkhanas and races at the Recreation ground. These annual shindigs were meant to boost morale and help families who were struggling to keep things normal, whilst loved ones were away from home and aiding the war effort. Many families had suffered bereavement too.

Anne dressed as Britannia in patriotic mode during a Fancy Dress event.

Children's sweet rations were supplemented by buying barley sugar and Horlicks tablets from the Chemists; by making toffee and toffee apples at home, or using lemonade crystals as 'sherbet'.

At Easter time Daddy would pierce an egg with a needle, blow out the egg and then pour melted chocolate into the hole. When the chocolate set the shell could be peeled off and this would reveal a chocolate egg, 'Real' Easter eggs weren't available during the war.

Our ration books were held at Palmers Stores, at the bottom of White Hart Street, opposite St Peter's Church

Mr Ben Palmer carefully supervised the allocation of groceries.

"Could you put by some jelly and blancmange powder, please. Anne is having a birthday party soon," Mummy would say.

Mr Palmer would consider the request for a moment, knowing that Mummy was hanging on his every word.

"Alright, Mrs Culey. I will. As long as you've got enough coupons saved up."

Pride of place at a children's party would be the pink or chocolate bunny, made in a mould, nestling amidst a bed of green grass jelly. During the war there was no ice cream and no bananas. We were made to eat bread and butter to fill us up before the wondrous blancmange could be tasted.

There were balloons and games such as 'Postman's Knock', 'Musical Chairs', 'Forfeits', 'Orange and Lemons' and many more.

Daddy was great fun at my parties, joining in the games and chasing us round the garden with a fur rug over his head calling,

"I'm a big spider and I'm coming to get you"

And we'd run away shrieking with fright and delight.

Soon there was to be further enchantment at Shrublands.

Chapter Twenty Seven

Our Exotic Land Girl

"Mummy, Daddy, I never, ever thought I'd have a bike!"

It was my seventh birthday and when I came home from school there it was, a green three wheeler, standing in the hall.

Anne on her new tricycle.

To make the day complete, my darling Iti had given me a Windsor and Newton paint box. My happiness was complete!

Iti, whose full title was Baroness Henrietta Perriera-Arnstein, had waltzed into our lives as an exotic creature, far more interesting than the men in blue or khaki uniforms who were billeted with us, even though some of them came from the far flung corners of the British Empire.

Iti had fled from Vienna when Austria had been annexed, in other words, taken over by Hitler. The name on her identity papers belied her Jewish origins and so, with the help of some English friends, Iti had escaped to England and enlisted in the Womens' Land Army. This organization had originally been formed during the First World War, as women took on the farming work of men who had enlisted in the forces.

Once in England Iti decided to call herself a Catholic but my parents knew and kept the secret, revealed in her papers when she had been sent to work as a Land Girl at Redgate Farm.

Because she was obviously 'a person of refinement' as Daddy put it, he and Mummy were reluctant to billet her with the other land girls in the more primitive sleeping arrangements at the farm. Some of the other land girls were a rough lot; having 'escaped' from northern industrial cities, they had chosen to work on farms as part of the war effort; as an alternative to slaving away in munitions factories but their language and behaviour were much coarser than Iti was used to.

This lovely, vivacious young woman brought a radiance to our lives. She was often amused and then her brown eyes shone with gaiety, her brown curls shook with mirth and she gave way to peals of laughter that echoed through the house.

Early each morning Iti donned the dark green jumper, the light brown corduroy breeches and tough beige socks that were the land girls' uniform and then she cheerfully cycled up to farm to milk the gentle Jersey cows.

Under her tutelage I learnt to paint quaint little Austrian chalets with fir trees beside them and moved on to wizened gnomes with bulbous noses and jutting eyebrows.

Iti bought me 'Uncle Peter's Russian Tales' and read them to me at night, as I lay in my little room with its wallpaper of 'Snow White and the Seven Dwarves'.

She introduced me to the music of Franz Lehar and the Strausses but she also liked playing records of Bing Crosby and I was soothed to sleep by the soft crooning of Bing's voice.

It wasn't long before Iti attracted admirers. American airmen were based at Wretham, Mildenhall and Lakenheath and local girls were invited to their Saturday night dances and taken by military trucks to the base.

I would enjoy watching Iti get ready for a night out, as she applied lipstick and powder and red stuff on her cheeks, which Mummy never used. She had made herself a pretty dirndl dress of cotton with a white lace edging along the low neckline.

Then Iti would get me to paint a thin straight line of brown right up the back of her tanned legs.

"It will look as if I hev stockings on, darlink," she would say.

We liked the fair, handsome New Englander she brought to see us. Gil, short for Gilchrist, flew Mustangs and he delighted us at harvest time by flying low over the wheat fields on Tut Hill Farm and performing daring 'loop the loops' for our entertainment. Gil was very taken with Iti but as her feelings for him grew stronger, he had to tell her that he would not break faith with his sweetheart Betty, back home in Massachusetts. And that was the end of the romance.

Iti and Gil at Shrublands.

Iti's next beau was a pilot called David Stein. He had a swarthy complexion and black hair that he sleeked down with some pungent oil. The smell of it lingered in a room long after he'd left. He tried to gain our favour with gifts of the 'new' nylon stockings and chocolates for Mummy and Hershey chocolate bars for me. Daddy thought him 'smarmy'.

One evening Iti and I were painting some Christmas cards in the kitchen. Mummy and Daddy had gone to a meeting at the Guildhall. They had said they would be back late and arranged for Iti to look after me.

The door bell rang and Iti went to answer it. I could hear her whispering to a man in the lobby, the conversation sounded urgent but they spoke in muffled tones.

Iti came into the kitchen, though I could glimpse the man hanging back in the shadows of the hall. I was sure it was David, although he didn't come in and say "Hi" to me, in his usual nasal drawl.

"Darlink" she said. "David and I are just going up to my room to talk some business. Will you be a very good girl and just get on with your painting down here for a while? I'll come down and make your Ovaltine later on but stay here won't you?"

I would do anything for Iti, so I promised to get on with my painting.

I painted a fir tree, a little white covered church with some people trudging to it through the snow.

Then I looked up at the clock. The long hand was on the 6. It had been on the 12 and the little hand on the 9 when they went upstairs. That was a long while. I should be in bed!

I crept to the bottom of the stairs and listened. There were noises coming from Iti's room. Not talking but a kind of muffled rhythm. Were they dancing? But there was no sound of Iti's Bing Crosby music. I was going to disobey Iti's request. I was worried, for as I climbed the stairs I heard Iti cry out. I rushed to her door and shouted. "Iti, Iti, are you allright?"

The door opened a crack. Iti's face was damp and hot, her hair was all over the place, her shoulders were bare.

At that moment I heard the front door opening.

Mummy and Daddy were home earlier than expected.

I ran downstairs, relieved that they were here.

"'Mummy, Mummy, I was doing my painting, like Iti said I should. I promised not to go upstairs because she said I should stay down here but I did go up 'cos it's bed time. I'm worried she might have a tummy ache because she was groaning and her face looked red."

When I came home from school next afternoon Mummy took my hand and said,

"Anne, dear, Iti's gone."

I thought my heart would break. I rushed upstairs to her room. Tears were blinding my eyes. The wide open window let in cold, cold air. The bed had been stripped. The wardrobe door was open wide; her lovely dresses, her Land Girl uniform, her records, her make up; all were gone. Only a hint of her perfume lingered. I burst into tears and flung myself onto the bed, burying my face into the pillow, then quickly recoiled and sat up in disgust because I could smell that man's sickly smelling hair oil on the pillow.

Later we heard that Iti had married an artist and gone to live in Chelsea. Sadly, on a motoring holiday in France after the war, her husband and one of their sons were killed, when they were involved in a car crash. I never saw Iti again, but like the music and her laughter, she has stayed in my memory.

Chapter Twenty Eight

The Turn of the Tide

Lovely Iti had arrived and suddenly left, just as the war was turning in our favour. The fact that the United States had finally joined the allies in the battle against Nazi Germany and Japan, had made a significant difference but their presence locally was a mixed blessing, as we saw from Iti's experience.

The fine quality of 'the Yanks' uniforms, their spending power and the presumed glamour of the land of opportunity, fuelled by Hollywood's films, caused friction between them and British servicemen. Fisticuffs would often break out in the town because their greater spending power gave them success with the local girls and put the lower paid British lads at a disadvantage.

The military police would be called out to stop fighting in the pubs.

The Americans easy friendliness and generosity endeared them to the public in general and particularly the young women but there were also false promises of a better life. Many girls who became GI brides discovered that life was not necessarily better on the other side of the Big Pond.

In my cosy bed at night I would hear the sound of drunken, raucous singing from the darkened alleys of the town as the troops bawled their favourite dirty song,

"Roll me over, in the clover" which began,

"This is number one and the fun has just begun,

Roll me over, lay me down and do it again"

At a very young age I had been introduced to a bawdy song about raw sex.

The popular American song "Over There" was rendered by our servicemen as,

"Over here, over here,

Overpaid, oversexed and over here."

During the war years members of Ben and Jessie's family and a friend had been killed. Jessie lost two of her cousins, Wilf and Reggie. They had died fighting in the jungles of Malaya, trying to hold back the advance of the Japanese soldiers towards Singapore. Those of their regiment, the Royal Norfolks who survived, spent the rest of the war incarcerated in the notorious Changi Gaol outside Singapore.

Ben Senior in Lynn, lost his sister, Florence Sharpin, killed by a bomb exploding directly onto her home in Boal Street, in the North End.

Our friend Bert Bullman, whose wife, Madge, had stayed with us at times during the war, had survived hostilities in North Africa but was killed when the plane bringing him home from Tunis crashed on take off. It was such a blow for his wife to lose him after the conflict had finished

I too felt his death keenly, for he wrote letters to me and I regarded him as 'my airman'. He had been more of a true 'Uncle' to me than my real Uncles.

I think he was fond of me because he and Madge had no children of their own.

In every letter he asked me to,

"Be a good girl for your Mummy and Daddy" and always signed himself 'Your Airman'.

Two of Daddy's cousins were more fortunate. They fought under Field Marshall Bernard Montgomery in the North African campaign and proudly wore the Desert Rats badge on the sleeve of their rough khaki jackets. They came home safely at the end of the war.

May 8th, 1945. I'm just home from school, playing on my swing at the end of the garden. Linga, who is home on leave, is pushing me higher and higher.

Mummy comes out from the house and calls to us excitedly,

"Anne, Linga, come up here. I've got some news!"

But she can't wait, she comes running toward us. "The war's over!" she cries.

We hug each other, jumping up and down with joy and the church bells start to ring all over the town.

Mummy takes me up to Savages, the haberdasher store on King Street. They are selling red, white and blue bunting and ribbons. Mummy buys some tricolour ribbon and ties bows on my plaits. Daddy finds some coloured lights in the garage and climbs a rickety ladder to fix them to the outside walls of the house.

A Victory dance is held at the Guildhall and I'm allowed to sit in the balcony and watch, even though it's way past my bed time.

August 8th 1945. Japan capitulates after atomic bombs are dropped on Nagasaki and Hiroshima. Now the Royal Norfolks, who have been held in Japanese prisoner of war camps, will be coming home.

This time we go over to Lynn to join in the celebrations with my grandparents.

Ben and Grace at Folly House had brought out the coloured lights and strung them around the monkey puzzle and other trees in their front garden, the upright piano was dragged onto the lawn and there was dancing for three nights, with free beer provided by my Granddad.

Folly House

After that they held two more parties in the Corn Exchange for the returning servicemen who were gradually being repatriated. About 400 men attended these parties. Ben senior deserved his reputation for generosity without stint.

Britain needed this time of celebration. Although peace returned to these islands, austerity, rationing, hardship and grief for lost loved ones, haunted our population for many years to come.

Chapter Twenty Nine

New Ventures

The end of the war brought many changes. Not only did Ben and Jessie find their home suddenly emptying of strangers but they decided to send their only child away from home as well.

I started boarding school at nine years old. I loved the company of girls my own age and sharing a dormitory with them but I missed the comfort of loving parents. And in winter I yearned for the warmth of having central heating, for there was none at school.

When I came home at the first half term I found Peter the pony had been sold, my dolls' house had disappeared and also my family of dolls; little Betty, my Chad Valley doll, named after Princess Elizabeth, Patsy, my coloured doll and Margaret, my German china doll. I was so glad that Edward Bear was safe with me at school.

When my parents realised how sad I was at what they'd done, they bought me a new Chad Valley doll but she hadn't shared my childhood and I didn't take to her.

Meanwhile Ben's thoughts were ever turning to new ventures. He had a restless mind and was only really fulfilled when he had a new project under way.

Jessie was a 'lark' and Ben was an 'owl'. Mummy would want everyone out of their beds at 7 30 am. An early cup of tea was one method of getting up 'lazy lie a beds'. Shortly after nudging the family in that way she would stand at the foot of the stairs and start calling persistently,

"Aren't you up YET?"

She dreaded the mornings when Ben had stayed up late the night before. He would tell her he was 'thinking'. and urge her,

"Go to bed Jess, I'll be up later."

Reluctantly she slowly climbed the stairs, leaving him to his thoughts and wondering what plans he was about to hatch.

Next morning he would lie in bed, secretly annoyed at the way she persisted in reading the 'EDP', the Eastern Daily Press, out loud to him, as she sat in bed next to him, sipping her tea. His brain was engaged on planning some new venture, with costings and sketches jotted on any envelope or piece of paper lying around.

Often Ben's schemes were revealed to Jessie after these ruminations; such as the time he suddenly announced,

"Guess what, Jessie, I'm going to buy Hanbury's Garage."

This was back in 1942, when Ben had suddenly decided it would be useful to own a garage, as he could then get the tractors and farm implements repaired on premises he owned. In fact he also bought Holmes' garage in Brandon with this in mind.

Hanbury's Garage stood on the corner of the main London Road out of Thetford, a good position for passing trade. However, petrol had been rationed throughout the war, so people couldn't travel very far on the allocation of their coupons; petrol for agricultural purposes was dyed orange, so that it couldn't be sold on the Black Market.

After the war the car industry was only slowly gaining momentum, as production of cars had been minimal during the conflict and petrol rationing continued. So although the garage's position was convenient for motorists topping up with petrol, the supply of new cars for sale was limited because the production lines were not yet operating fully.

Ben had to adhere to a strict system imposed by the new government and kept a waiting list of people wanting cars. Some people got very annoyed if they had to wait more than a year, which was usual at the time and many of them tried to 'persuade' Ben to let them have a car before it was their turn.

Ben was soon frustrated. By nature he was not a patient man and disliked the restrictions.

To get away from it for a while, he took us to Switzerland by train in early January, 1946. Used to the privations of war, we were enchanted by the elegant dining car with its pristine white cloths, the fine china, black cherry jam and pure white bread. As we enjoyed our afternoon tea, the panoramic windows gave us a view of the snow covered Engadine mountains, tipped with pink at sunset.

We were amazed by the plentitude of chocolate and patisserie shops in St Moritz and ate so many fancy cakes that our stomachs, unused to rich food, rebelled.

Ben and Anne on skis in St Moritz.

Ben hadn't skied before but was determined to have a go. So he bought a pair of skis and set off down the main street of St Moritz. It was a steep hill and Ben was going too fast. He could not control his speed. There were people walking in front of him and he was afraid he would collide with them. In desperation he grabbed hold of a man round his substantial middle, to act as a break to his calamitous speed. In great surprise the man was twirled round in the collision and Ben began apologising profusely.

The man shook his head in bewilderment. He couldn't understand a word Ben was saying. At last he realised that Ben was English. His puzzled expression changed to one of amusement. He smiled and shook Ben by the hand.

Ben picked up his ski poles and tentatively edged his way back to the hotel.

He would try out his new skis in a less public place next time.

At that time visitors to Europe were only allowed to take £25 out of the country.

I am not sure how we managed to have a holiday on that amount?

Another amusing incident took place on a motoring holiday to Sweden and Norway. Instead of a 'drive on' ferry, the few cars that travelled were

173

picked up by crane and deposited on the deck. Watching our car swinging to and fro on iron chains above the dock was quite scary.

At a hotel in Karlsbad, Sweden an American woman took a great liking to Ben and pursued him, which caused great embarrassment, as Jessie became more and more irritated by the woman's relentless presence and her questions. She asked Jessie;

"So why do people refer to your husband as 'The General'? Is he a REAL General?"

"Oh yes," Jessie replied, thinking fast. "He is. He's a General in the Salvation Army."

Her answer was a brainwave.

'The General' was an affectionate nickname someone had given to Ben but Jessie's little fib resulted in the American hastily leaving the hotel dining room. Ben wasn't bothered by her attentions again. Privately he may have wondered where she had gone so abruptly!

These excursions abroad were a mere diversion to the problems Ben was facing with Hanbury's garage and it wasn't long after that Ben confessed something to Jessie, self conciously clearing his throat, as he always did before a big announcement.

"I think I made a mistake Jess, taking on Hanbury's. I'm not really cut out for the rigmarole and putting people on waiting lists of over a year."

It came as no surprise to Jessie that Ben had decided to give up his interest in the garage business. He managed to sell it to a firm called Nice. Jessie was so relieved. She thought it was a 'nice' move as far as Ben was concerned.

Chapter Thirty

Messing about in Boats

Just like Ratty in 'Wind in the Willows', Ben's inheritance from the fisher folk of his family meant that he loved to be on or near water, whether it be the River Ouse, or the Thet, or the great North Sea, despite his tendency to suffer sea sickness in rough conditions.

There was always a small dinghy in the boat shed at the bottom of the garden at 'Shrublands' and from the time I was seven my own clinker built rowing boat was tied up by the landing stage with 'Anne Bridget' proudly painted in gold lettering on its hull. My father taught me to wield the heavy wooden oars and soon I was rowing up the Thet as far as the Melford Bridge Tavern and back.

In those days rivers was regularly dredged for weeds, so that wild life flourished in the stream and on the river banks. Ben preferred 'a bit more speed' and favoured outboard motors or speed boats. He enjoyed inviting young chaps aboard and 'testing them for their mettle' by revving the engine and executing risky turns at high speed dangerously close to the bank, to see if they showed signs of pluck or cowardice.

Jessie looked on from the bay windows, 'tutt-tutting ' in disapproval at Ben's antics.

Shortly after the end of World War Two, Ben learnt that the Admiralty were selling off the motor launches that had been built for high speed patrols along the East Coast to chase off enemy craft.

Large numbers of these launches were now obsolete to the nation's requirements and were laid up at Gillingham, on the River Medway in Kent.

Ben attempted to mention his intentions in a low key way.

"Jess," he said, clearing his throat. "I think I'd like to go down to Gillingham and take a look at those M.L.s."

Jessie knew her Ben only too well and as she waved goodbye to him as he roared up the lane in the family car, she worried, "What's he getting up to now?"

Her question was soon answered. The very next day she had a phone call.

"Hello Darling,' Ben said, rather cautiously.

"Well" and here he paused rather sheepishly, "I've had a look and um, I've bought one!" Here he couldn't help sounding a bit pleased with himself.

"Oh no Ben," groaned an exasperated Jessie "What on earth are you going to do with it?"

"Its number is ML549."

Ben was heedless of her question. His enthusiasm was spilling over.

"I'm having the Fairmile petrol engines replaced with diesels. Then I'll get Bill Beniffer to bring it round to Lynn."

The sale was completed on 26th April 1946, between the Director of Small Craft Disposals, by order of the Admiralty and Benjamin C Culley (sic) for the sum of £145 and10 shillings.

Bill Beniffer belonged to one of the fishing families in Lynn and lived in Pilot Street. Together with Bill's brother and another 'old salt' called Tipney Goodson, the three of them, with Ben, who had hardly any knowledge of seamanship, successfully brought the craft safely from Gillingham, round the Essex, Suffolk and Norfolk coastline to the Alexandra Dock in Lynn.

Melanie proceeding along 'The Cut' to King's Lynn docks.

Here it went an extensive 'fitting out', as the Navy would term it. A deck cabin was added and the cabins were upgraded.

Jessie and Ben decided to name their new craft 'Melanie' for they had recently seen the musical "Perchance to Dream" by Ivor Novello, in London's West End. The name was painted on the bows.

Unfortunately Lloyds of London informed Ben that the name 'Melanie' had already been registered as a vessel's name. This was a pity. Not only had the name 'Melanie' already been applied to the bows but Ben, in his usual impulsive style, had written to the actress playing 'Melanie' and received a photo from her inscribed "Happy sailing to MY Melanie".

The leading lady, Melanie, 'We'll gather lilacs'.

So they chose the name of the second character in the musical, and their new possession was officially named ML 'Melinda'.

It was only a year since the war had ended and there were not the number of pleasure boats that we are used to seeing in harbours and marinas around the coasts of Britain. Melinda's elegant lines caused quite a stir amongst onlookers.

Ben, like his father was always generous and shared his good fortune with others.

The Culey gift for hospitality meant that the family, a wide circle of friends and organisations from Thetford and Lynn were invited for days out on the Wash with 'Melinda'.

Ben Culey senior and Ben Culey junior 'taking the mick' out of his dad (he wasn't a smoker).

It often meant an early morning start to catch the tide and it was thrilling to set out at dawn, to move smoothly and silently along the silver grey Ouse and enter the expanses of the Wash, to the sad sound of the seagulls' cries and the calls of other sea birds. We watched seals basking on sand banks, looking up in surprise as we invaded their territory then saw them slipping clumsily into the water to head away from such a strange beast.

178

The crew of Melinda, Bill Beniffer in boiler suit, 'Tipney' Goodson in a 'gansey', Doris Braime (cook) and Walter Braime on far right.

With time Ben grew more adventurous.

"Let's take her round the coast, Jess. You've always enjoyed Torquay. We could make a holiday of it and take some of your family."

So, gaining Jessie's reluctant agreement, in the summer of 1949, Melinda set sail for the South coast. Members of the crew included the Beniffer brothers, one of them acting as engineer, Walter and Doris Braime, who came as cook, Kenny Armes from the farm, along with Lewis Means, who helped plot the course. Jessie and her sisters Gracie and Cassie, Willie White her brother, my cousins Margaret and Bridget and me.

Our first port of call was Great Yarmouth, which we managed within a day.

One little girl on the quayside asked in amazement;

"Can you stand up as the boat travels along and can you really stay on board at night?"

This was before the days of television when children learn so much about the world. She had never seen a boat 'for living on' before.

The younger members of our party loved the freedom of being allowed to walk along the quay in a gang and buy a bag of chips for a threepenny bit. The chips would be wrapped in a twist of newspaper.

The second night of our adventure we docked at Dover and then we continued along the South coast towards Poole.

As we passed through the channel between the Isle of Wight and Portsmouth we became aware of people on another vessel waving to us frantically,

"Gosh, they r'e very friendly,"I innocently remarked to my cousins.

Ben was standing on the bridge.

"What's up?" he called out through his loud hailer.

"Sand banks!" roared the crew on the other vessel.

Bill Beniffer our skipper, called for depth readings over the side with the plumb line and then he carefully changed course and edged Melinda out of the shallow water. So much for novices using a chart without proper qualifications.

At each quayside we were surrounded by curious holiday makers, for in those days of austerity, people weren't used to seeing private pleasure craft in any numbers and certainly not the glitzy 'gin palaces' that would herald increasing prosperity for some.

At last we reached Torquay and stayed for a week.

Going ashore from Melinda.

When it was time for the return voyage Jessie went ahead by train with little Bridget, who was only six. All was calm sailing until the morning we were due to sail on the final leg of our journey from Great Yarmouth to Lynn.

The sea was rough and capped by dancing 'white horses'. The skies looked ominously grey and heavy with rainclouds.

A storm was brewing.

Ben, ever the optimist, decided to brave the storm. As we edged towards the harbour entrance a Naval vessel heading into port flashed a signal to us,

"Do NOT proceed."

"Blow that" said Ben and ordered the skipper, Bill Beniffer, to carry on.

Before long we were in open water and being buffeted by enormous waves. The wind was fierce and my cousin Margaret and I retreated to the deck cabin for safety.

"Would it be better to go back or carry on?"

Ben asked Bill, for he was already feeling mighty sea sick.

"Oh well" said the phlegmatic Bill, used to stormy seas." We might as well carry on now. Once we've rounded the corner we'll get into calmer waters."

'The corner' was the top bulge of Norfolk's coast, where we would turn into the more protected waters of the Wash.

The storm grew in strength. The ship was rearing and bucking like a wild horse. The seas were tumultuous and the sky merged with the sea until visibility was nil.

My cousin and I were terrified and cowered in the cabin, clutching each other in fright. The adults aboard were too busy trying to keep Melinda on an even keel to see to us.

They were probably as scared as we were.

We heard Melinda's engine roar as she climbed to the top of each huge wave and then took a sickening vertiginous tumble down into a trough before struggling to the top of the next gigantic wave.

Were we going to die?

By keeping a cool head the skipper brought us round the coast into the familiar, calmer waters of the Wash and safely up to the Alexandra dock in Lynn.

Never would we be more grateful to step on to dry land.

As we all emerged from the wheelhouse, the deck house and below decks, there were chalk white faces and queasy stomachs. To our great surprise Mrs Braime had cooked a hearty stew in the galley during that fearful storm and we were even more surprised that we could tuck into it with a good appetite, now that our ordeal was over.

As we ate, the skipper informed us,

"Dew yew know those waves were thirty foot high and water wuz a' comin' down the funnel?"

Did this extreme experience influence Ben's decision to sell 'Melinda' soon after? He knew that 'Melinda' and her sister ships had been built of cheap marine plywood in the rush to counter enemy attacks around the East coast and he surmised 'Melinda' would fall prey to woodworm very soon.

He placed an advertisement in 'The Yachting World'.

To his surprise a 'Mr Smeeth' (for that is how the gentleman with such a very English name pronounced it, in a suspiciously foreign sounding accent) rang Ben after seeing the advert and quickly arranged for his agent to come and inspect 'Melinda'.

"He was really only interested in how fast she could go. All he looked at was her powerful diesel engines," Ben remarked to Jessie after the inspection had taken place.

Some months later he discovered the agent's motive for the keen interest in 'Melinda's speed.

It was breakfast time at Shrublands and a surprised and embarrassed Jessie silently passed the newspaper to Ben. She couldn't believe her eyes. It took her breath away. There in the Daily Express was the story of how the new owner of a former M L, once owned by the Royal Navy, had been arrested for smuggling.

He had operated an illegal racket between the ports of Spain and Morocco. The craft had been impounded and now languished in some foreign port. The mysterious 'Mr Smeeth' was found to be a fraud.

What an ignoble end for our patriotic 'Melinda'.

Chapter Thirty One

"That on't work hare"

On Redgate Farm there had been two foot and mouth outbreaks amongst the cattle. The sight of the lovely Jersey cattle burning on a funeral pyre must have been heart breaking for Ben.

Then fowl pest spread like wild fire through the chickens packed in tightly caged battery houses. Ben had bought the battery houses after the war, seeing it as a way to keep more birds, and thus increase egg production. It was dreadful to see the poor creatures cooped up and picking out each others feathers in distress. I was not sorry to know that the battery houses were sold after the second outbreak of fowl pest.

For my father to see all the affected cows, all the affected chickens destroyed by fire must have seemed like the end of his dreams for expanding business after the war.

Though Ben started his businesses with optimism, he was desolate when things went wrong and so he started to look for other ways to make a living.

In the early 1950s there was a growing need for more housing and Ben, disheartened by his bad luck at Redgate Farm, decided to sell the land to a builder who was interested in the site. The builder had caught Ben on the back foot after his losses and seized his opportunity to buy at a low price.

In Ben's view he packed too many houses and bungalows onto the site. People living there seemed quite happy with their new bungalows but Ben had anticipated the site would be better planned. Too late he remarked to Jessie,

"If only I'd designed and built the estate myself, I wouldn't have crowded them so close."

Alas, there were more down turns and 'if only's' to follow.

Never a man to be discouraged for long, Ben thought about what else was needed to move Thetford forward into a bright post war future. As usual, Jessie was a little alarmed and dismayed by his late night ruminations.

"Jessie, what this town needs is somewhere for the youngsters to meet, instead of them hanging around street corners."

"Oh Ben, what do you have in mind NOW," she sighed as she wearily turned on her side and tried to sleep.

Ben, oblivious to her sighs, chuntered on;

"Well, I'm going to see old Dick Goddard. I hear he's selling off the Mecca cafe on King Street. I'll go and see him in the morning."

His friend, Dick Goddard, who also owned Goddards and Son, the building firm, owned a small cafe called 'The Mecca', half way down Kings Street, Thetford's main shopping street; the cafe was a bit old fashioned, and slightly run down, like most of the eating places in Thetford after the war.

Ben bought it and made it into Thetford's first Milk Bar in the style of an American ice cream parlour, where milk shakes and ice cream sundaes could be consumed, whilst sitting on high stools by the long bar. Ben also installed an Italian coffee machine with flashing lights and a great deal of noise, so that Thetford youngsters could enjoy lattes and cappuccinos, long before these became commonplace. Ben had seen them in some of the new coffee bars that were springing up in London near Wardour Street, when he went up to order films.

There was also a juke box. Ben installed others in various pubs and collected 'the takings' every week.

Thetford 'teenagers', a description that was only just coming into use, took to the milk bar in a big way. It was officially named 'The Rendezvous,' following a competition at the cinema to choose a name; though being the only one in Thetford it was more commonly referred to like this;

"Cum on. I ent a-doin narthin t'noight, les's go down the Milk Bar un meet sum uv are mearts".

It soon became a favourite meeting place where boys and girls could make an ice cream soda last at least a couple of hours.

Cissie Scott was the manager aided by one or two younger girls

When I was about fifteen years old, Dad 'allowed' me to work there on Saturdays for the meezly sum of 2/6d, the equivalent of about 30p today!

Boys would come in and tell me their problems, just as barmaids in pubs are often the confidantes of lonely drinkers. One of the lads was called Valentine and another was Tom, an aspiring reader to whom I enjoyed lending books. When Ben realised that boys were coming into the milk bar to 'chat up' his daughter, rather than to buy drinks, he soon stopped me from going there any more.

Being a wily business man Ben set up his own ice cream making plant at the rear of the building and under the trade name of Midland ice cream, it was made daily. Then at the end of the day the surplus would be run off and eager youngsters would collect in Giles Lane for free hand outs of the white stuff.

The building next to the Milk Bar fell vacant and Ben seized the opportunity to extend his catering enterprise.

The Anglian Cafe and Restaurant was created for a more affluent clientele.

"We'll have to do it proper, Jess. Hire a chef through an agency and have the waitresses dressed up, like them Lyons House 'nippies' in their neat black dresses and little white aprons with frills; oh and little white caps on their heads. You can help me design the interior. Nice tables with white cloths, comfortable dining chars, not cheap ones."

Ben's mind was once again running ahead of him.

"Oh Ben!" thought Jessie, "Why does it always have to be the best of everything, eating into our income."

Jessie had inherited the more frugal attributes of her father and tried to curb the excesses of the Culey mind set.

"Why the most expensive voile curtains at the window? Why do we have to have the inevitable Culey style aquarium with tropical fish, needing unnecessary attention and upkeep?"

A lot of the women recruited were known to Ben through 'doubling up' as usherettes at the cinema.

The opening in 1950 was, in true Culey style, heralded by a big fanfare of celebrity appearances. It fortuitously tied in with the Festival of Britain and as part of the celebrations Ben hired Roberto Taylor's Rumba Band from London to play on a float advertising the Anglian Cafe. Ben had heard them playing at the Churchill Club. The locals ogled the glamorous South American dark eyed beauty, whose sultry voice accompanied the band. It was a great success.

Tom Jenkins, the violinist from the BBC show 'Sunday Night with Tom Jenkins and his Palm Court Orchestra' also gave a recital at The Anglian Restaurant.

He didn't bring the orchestra, only his accompanist on the piano. He was a gentle Welshman and Ben and Jessie entertained him overnight at Shrublands.

Ben, with his expertise for booking films would have known how to get hold of these artists through their agents in London.

Whilst mentioning long gone celebrities, Franklin Engleman of the BBC's 'Down your Way' came to Thetford and, on a bright summer's afternoon, interviewed Ben in the garden of Shrublands.

Another visitor was Adrian Brunel. The film producer and grandson of the famous railway engineer Isambard Kingdom Brunel, stayed with Jessie and Ben for a few days, to explore the town, with a view to making a film about the town's controversial son, Thomas Paine. The flamboyant Mr Brunel was a great admirer of Tom Paine and sadly, though he and also the late Richard Attenborough both wanted to bring the ideas and writings of the great man to life on screen, the project has never come to fruition. Did Adrian Brunel hope to find local funding for the scheme and was this the real reason for his visit?

The film producer gave Ben a copy of his memoir "My Life in Pictures' and gave me a copy of Robert Browning's poems, a man he also admired.

Then he left and we never heard from him again.

The Anglian Restaurant and Milk Bar, Jessie Culey at entrance.

186

Ben was proud of 'The Anglian Restaurant' and for a man who knew nothing about the catering business beforehand, he made an important contribution to the social life of the town in providing the Milk Bar for the youngsters and the restaurant for couples and families. When he talked about it in later years he would remember;

"A full three course meal cost 3/6d. Why, a whole Dover sole cost only 5 shillings. Of course, there was still food rationing at the time, so it was good that people could get a meal out without 'coupons'.

Children's parties and anniversaries were catered for in the room upstairs but although the cost of meals was reasonable, Thetfordians were not yet accustomed to having meals in restaurants. Unfortunately this was a case of Ben being ahead of his time. If only he could have gone into this business twenty years later, when people had more money in their pockets!

A gloomy Ben heads home.

"What's the matter, dear?" enquires an anxious Jessie, "You look done in."

"I am." Ben replies angrily.

"I've just had to sack that ruddy Chef of ours, Murphy. I've suspected him for some time but looking into the accounts I've found out he's a wrong 'un."

"Why, what's he done?" asked a fearful Jessie,

She'd always sensed Mr Murphy was not what he purported to be. Maybe he'd run off with one of the waitresses? She'd never liked the florid, over effusive Irishman.

"He's been drinking our profits, that's what he's done. Why he was so drunk he was making passes at the women. Not to mention pocketing the takings. Someone like him would soon ruin our reputation, let alone the business".

Ben himself was almost a 'teetotaller' and had no respect for people who fell prey to alcohol. But the worst part was that his trust in someone had been misplaced.

The staff on the farms, the cinemas, the milk bar and restaurant had always been like a family. Ben and Jessie were good employers. They treated their staff with respect and kindness.

In appreciation of their loyal service Ben and Jessie took all their staff on an annual outing to Great Yarmouth, to the Hippodrome and to a meal afterwards. In those days it was a good day out. Very rarely did 'The Boss' come across 'a bad egg'. So when the couple were let down by Mr Murphy they took it badly.

In time Ben had to face up to the fact that the restaurant and the milk bar were not making a profit, even though the thieving manager had been sacked.

So he sold them both.

As Norfolk humourist Sidney Grapes would comment through the medium of his 'Aunt Agatha'; "No matter what happen, there's always someone knew it would."

One of the delights of my teenage years was going up to Wardour Street, London with my Dad, if he felt in the mood to order films directly, rather than through the film 'travellers' who regularly came to our house.

"B-e e-e-n" The small, rotund man sounded the name in a long drawn out call; holding his arms wide and beaming at my father, as he came rushing down the curving marble staircase of Warner Brothers offices.

"It's good to see you" he said, clasping my dad in a bear hug, as if he were some long lost cousin. The gold rings on his chubby fingers glittered and his gold teeth shone.

I think my father let David think that he might be Jewish in order to give their bargaining a better chance. Benjamin wasn't then the generally popular name it has become.

Cordiality is one thing; business is another. Prolonged bargaining followed as the two men sweated at some tough negotiations in David's stuffy office, with the London traffic noises resonating from the street below.

It was difficult to book specific films by name at reasonable prices, which is why Dad thought it worth paying a visit to 'headquarters' to see if he could get a better deal.

At the end of a tough, gruelling time, David would slap Ben on the back with a "Goodbye, my friend" and see us off the premises in great good humour.

As a 'treat' for waiting quietly, Dad would take me to Leon's Chinese Restaurant, close by in Soho and after gorging on succulent and authentic Chinese dishes my father would burp loudly, lean across the table and whisper,

"You must burp, Anne. The Chinese consider it an affront or criticism of the meal if you don't show your satisfaction by burping."

I don't think my mother would have thought it a good thing to burp under any circumstances. But it was always good fun to be out with my Dad!

Chapter Thirty Two

Lights out at Lynn

Whilst Ben was dealing with business problems in Thetford, his father in Lynn was struggling with declining health.

"Bennie, you'd better get over here quick. Dad's had a stroke."

Grace was desperate for her son's support.

When 'young' Ben arrived, his father couldn't speak and one side of his face had dropped.

A second stroke followed and he died.

Trying to be helpful, Ben blurted out,

"Just as well he went that way, Mother. He had cancer of the stomach."

The body was embalmed and placed in the sitting room. The coffin was left open and according to the custom of the time people visited Folly House to pay their last respects to the deceased.

I was encouraged to,

"Go and kiss your Granddad goodbye".

I didn't really want to, I had never seen a dead person before.

'Why is he wearing make up?' I asked myself, not knowing that this was the way dead people were prepared for burial then.

On the day of the funeral I was given pride of place and sat in the first of the black limousines, beside Grandma. As the car moved smoothly behind the hearse along the drive she began to wail,

"Oh Ben, my Ben, why are you leaving me? I can't bear it".

She lunged forward, reaching towards the hearse in her agony.

The procession moved along Wootton Road at a dignified pace on the two mile journey to St Margaret's Parish Church. All the way there the pavements were lined with people, standing silent and respectful. Men doffed their caps or raised their trilby hats, women bowed their heads as we passed by. Policemen stood to attention at intervals along the route. I noticed black mourning boards in shop windows. In this way the owners honoured a much loved character, who'd become known as "The man with the Midas touch."

As we walked solemnly into St Margaret's Church behind the coffin we could see, out of the corner of our eyes, that the large church was packed with mourners.

Grace didn't get over the loss of Ben. They had shared fifty years of a passionate, vibrant, argumentative life together and she suddenly lost her zest for living.

During that winter she was admitted to the London Clinic with pneumonia. This was during one of the London 'smogs' and I remember wearing a mask to filter out the yellowish pollution as I travelled through London to visit her.

Grace returned home but she was much diminished, even though the 'hangers on' still clustered around her.

Then she developed bronchitis. I went to say 'goodbye' for she was fading fast. Her breathing was laboured and her face was grey. I held her damp hand and her pale blue eyes searched my face.

"Anne dear, do you want a glass of milk?" Those were her last words to me. To the last she was typically thinking of others, even though she was desperately ill herself.

Jessie caught the 'hangers on' rifling through Grace's jewellery cabinet when they thought no one was in the room.

"What are you lot doing? What a rotten lot you are. Go on, clear off and don't come back!"

This sent them scurrying away. Ben was amazed at the way his usually mild Jessie had sent them packing.

"Why they're like a huddle of carrion crows" she snapped.

In their later years Grace and Ben had been given poor financial advice and so Folly House had to be sold immediately to pay death duties. My father had tried to protect his mother from the problems he'd faced in attempting to sell the house and its extensive grounds after Ben senior had died. The property market was sluggish in the mid fifties. No one wanted a large house with extensive gardens. Eventually a developer bought the house and pulled it down to make room for a small estate of very mundane houses. Not only the spacious Edwardian house and conservatory came down but also the beautiful weeping ash tree, the monkey puzzle and other specimen trees. The lily ponds, green houses and Grace's lovely flower beds were all destroyed.

Grace's little Victorian girl from her garden

Ben died in1954 but the Pilot Cinema sailed on under the management of family trustees. In 1961 Malcolm Croote took over as manager.

There were highlights, such as 'The Sound of Music' in 1967, when 40,000 people came to see it. There were coach loads from Norwich, Peterborough and Skegness and other towns in Lincolnshire and Norfolk.

In the 1970s 'Jaws' was being shown and such a gale arose that the roof blew off, which terrified the audience even more than the scary film.

But not even great films could stem the relentless decline in cinema attendance as people relied more on 'the box in the corner' for their entertainment. The Pilot finally closed its doors in 1983 after a showing of 'Ghandi,' a great film and a noble ending for a fine cinema.

The auditorium was packed and at the end the audience stood in silent homage; to the film and also in tribute to the cinema that had been so much a part of their lives.

Having served as a garden centre and a night club called 'Zoots', it succumbed to other uses.

The grand old building has recently been demolished and housing has been built there.

Edna, Grace and Ben in the garden of Folly House

Chapter Thirty Three

Fortune Falters

There is a saying that 'Fortune favours the brave'. This rang true when Ben Culey was young, optimistic and ready to 'do diff'runt'.

Just as his father had been labelled in Lynn as, 'The man with the Midas touch,' when everything seemed to go his way, it seemed as if Ben's life in Thetford was also blessed with good fortune.

However, by 1966 Ben was sixty years old and the full tide of his life was ebbing.

He had suffered set backs in farming through swine fever and fowl pest and the resulting sale of Redgate Farm had depressed him as 'a failure'. He was not used to failing on such a large scale and his abundant optimism and energy flagged.

Hanbury's Garage had been sold. The Milk Bar and the Anglian Restaurant had not been a commercial success. Although he had renovated the cinema; introducing the Candy Box for the sale of sweets, chocolates, ice cream and cigarettes, even putting a juke box in the foyer and a delicatessen at the front, it was a step too far for Thetford.

Of course people flocked to the free performance at the opening of the improvements but soon their curiosity was satisfied and many returned to seeing the very latest releases in Bury St Edmunds at the Odeon. Married people with families stayed at home and watched television. Cinemas were no longer needed as the main source of entertainment.

The new craze was 'Bingo' Should he go down this road?

"I always wanted to give people good value for their money" he said to his friends.

"Getting people to come to the cinema to play Bingo is taking people's money and giving very little in return."

In this argument there is a hint of his mother Grace's condemnation of any form of gambling. Her son Ben never gambled himself, as he had seen the devastating effects it had had in his sister Edna's life with Percy.

With a heavy heart he realised that if Bingo was what people wanted, he could not bring himself to provide it for them.

Cliff Waterman was keen to set up a place for Bingo in Thetford and so it was decided he would hire the Palace from Ben from 1966 and have Bingo on two nights of the week. Geoffrey High was appointed manager and Freda Howard stayed on as cashier. This rental of the cinema continued for ten years.

In 1976 Ben Culey sold both the Palace in Thetford and the Avenue in Brandon to Cliff Waterman and the ensuing business became known as Breckland Cinemas.

The state of the cinema during those final ten years makes a sorry tale of vandalism, neglect and lack of upkeep. The closure in the summer of 1985 of the cinema in Thetford, with only fifteen people attending the final showing of 'Romancing the Stone' is no surprise.

From that date the building was totally turned over to the pursuit of Bingo.

Then in 2008 Cliff Waterman sold both buildings on to the Independent Winners Bingo Club. The Palace still exists as a Bingo Hall. The Avenue cinema has been allowed to slowly moulder away to a ruin and is to be pulled down and replaced by housing.

Chapter Thirty Four

Civic, Community and Masonic Matters

Ben Culey was not just interested in his various business ventures. Although the personal lives of his father and 'young Ben,' were always filled with incident, it is only right that this chapter should address the importance he placed on his public duties.

Until he was in his eighties Ben was deeply involved in public issues and speaking his mind forcefully in the interests of Thetford. This interest in the town sprung from his desire to make Thetford a better place to live. Back in those days councillors didn't receive any financial assistance with their work

He became an independent candidate and came top of the poll at the age of 30 in 1937.

He was elected Mayor of Thetford on three separate occasions, firstly in 1949, then during a busy period of expansion from 1968 to1970.

One of Ben's election leaflets.

His success as Mayor lay in his ability to deal with people from all walks of life, his sociability, persuasiveness and business acumen. Despite his lack of knowing German he endeared himself to the people of Hurth on visits with the Fire Service. He was made an 'honorary' fireman.

Because of his humour and good will the people of Hurth nicknamed him 'Mr Wunderbar'.

Rhinelanders in general have the same positive, cheerful outlook on life as Ben did.

He was a founding member of the Thetford's Rotary Club and soon took on the mantle of president.

He was a member of numerous Masonic Lodges and Chapters and gave generously to their charities.

For several years he served as a Justice of the Peace in Thetford and was known for his benign judgements on miscreants.

He was so proud of his work on the waterworks committee and oversaw the drilling of a deep bore to provide Thetford with good quality drinking water.

He was president of the Dolphins Swimming Club and loved urging them on in competitions and travelling to Europe with them. There were Ben and Jessie cups awarded to the best swimmers each year.

Ben was a governor at several Thetford schools and took a keen interest in them.

He was active in the Chamber of Commerce and once again presented a Culey cup for the best window display. A cup that was stolen. Was it ever recovered?

He loved his adopted town and did all he could to promote its interests.

In the 1950s the Borough Council appointed a small sub committee formed of three business men belonging to the Chamber of Commerce to promote Thetford's growth and prosperity. One was Mr John Wilson who represented a cheese company, so John became known as 'Cheesy' Wilson. The second committee member was Mr Cooper, manager of Twinings Ibex Coffee Company. The Coffee Mill, as it was commonly called, was situated on the side of Shrubland's land and the 'tap tap tap' of the engine and the delicious smell of coffee permeated my early years. My father, Ben Culey, as a local business man with a finger in many pies, was the third member of the committee.

Mr Cooper, a Londoner, suggested approaching London County Council, who were keen to 'export' some of London's burgeoning population to the provinces.

The London County Council was looking for towns willing to undertake expansion and Thetford's Town Clerk, Ellis Clarke, formally invited the London County Council to send a delegation to Thetford. The party was headed by Mrs Evelyn Dennington, Chairman of the LCC's Expanding Towns Committee.

The Mayor, of Thetford, the afore mentioned John Wilson and the LCC party, were wined and dined at the Anglian cafe, where the champagne flowed freely, thanks to Ben's lavish hospitality. The LCC party exclaimed;

"This is the best reception we've had in any town" and soon decided, after perhaps a rather befuddled look around the town, to sign an agreement for expansion.

Many Thetfordians once more muttered "that on't work hare". Just as they'd derided the idea of a 'posh' restaurant, they argued that Thetford, almost ninety miles from London, was too distant and that Londoners would not want to move away from what they knew; but the plan went ahead because the manufacturing companies wanted it. Thermos moved their factory to the town, Conran, Jeyes, Danepak, Baxters Laboratories, also a company that processed woodchip and many more. New estates were built to house the 'incomers'. Fortunately many Londoners were keen to make a fresh start in the clean air of Norfolk and quickly adapted to their new life in Thetford. After all, they moved with their source of work and therefore with their friends and work mates.

The word for this upheaval became the rather derogatory one of 'overspill'. Perhaps it went further than the instigators envisaged, especially with the pulling down of historic buildings in the town centre and replacing them with ugly 1960s 'brutalist' style concrete buildings, including the infamous Carnegie Rooms, a building that was part funded by the Andrew Carnegie trust and has since needed unending repair.

Whereas councillors who valued Thetford's historic buildings were dismayed by the pillage of the old town, Ben Culey was always a man looking to the future and he was able to embrace the changes.

'Howsomever,' as Norfolk people say, all the downsides of these optimistic ventures lay in the future and at the time the decisions were made there were high hopes for Thetford's growth and prosperity.

When Ben was elected Mayor for the third time he and Jessie spent every weekend greeting the coach loads of Londoners coming down from London and giving them a guided tour of their new home town.

Alongside this active promotion of the town Ben got involved in the Town Twinning projects; with Spikenisee in the Netherlands, Hurth, an industrial town near Cologne in West Germany and Boo, a town in Sweden, which later backed out of the arrangement.

Ben loved welcoming the deputations and entertaining them. He also enjoyed the return visits, especially at the time of the Rose Monday Carnival in Cologne, when he would happily put on fancy dress in keeping with the occasion and join the parades in the streets. The happy-go-lucky Rhinelanders took my father to their hearts as one of their own kind and Ben and Jessie became close friends with some of the people they met. . The language barrier meant nothing to them. I have already mentioned how his open heartedness earned him the nick name 'Mr Wunderbar' (Mr Wonderful) because his favourite expression was,

"This is wonderful!'

Ben at the Rose Montag Carnival in Cologne.

It was probably the highlight of Ben's public life to be awarded the 'Ehrenring', the ring of friendship, which meant he was given the freedom of Hurth. Not many 'foreigners' were accorded this honour; in fact the only person to have received it before my father was the Russian president, Mr Gorbachov.

Ben with his Ehren ring.

To get the right size gold ring made for Ben in Germany, Jessie had to send the ring off the garden hose pipe, as it was the only thing she could find big enough to give them an idea of the width of his fourth finger.

Yet it was not only in the big matters that my father promoted Thetford.

Once I was out with him in the town and a man wound down the window of his car and asked for directions.

"Hold on," said Dad, after unsuccessfully trying to explain the route through Thetford's winding streets. There was no Sat Nav in those days.

"I'll get my car and you can follow me" he told the man. So then he drove through the town to the outskirts with the stranger following him.

"Why on earth did you go to all that trouble?" I asked him.

"Well, Anne," he replied,

"A gesture like that means they'll remember our little town and have a good impression of it."

Some of Dad's exploits showed elements of the dare devil in him.

He took Ellis Clarke, who was Thetford's Town Clerk, to the Farnborough Air Show. Dad was fond of speed: he loved to watch the race track events at Snetterton. He loved fast cars, speed boats and aeroplanes.

Having arrived near the airfield, Ben saw a very long queue of cars lining the road as far as he could see, all waiting to get through the entrance gates. . Dad was impatient, for the show had begun.

"Come on Ellis" he said and parked the car close to the hedge. Then the two of them scrambled through the wire fence to get into the grounds. It must have been an amusing sight, for Ellis was a very tall, lanky man and Ben was a short, stout one.

"What would people think?" Ellis said, when he told the story, "To see the Mayor and Town Clerk of the Ancient Borough of Thetford, clambering through a wire barrier and committing an act of trespass. What if we'd been accosted by the law? It doesn't bear thinking about. What a headline in the popular press!"

One thing Ben was utterly serious about was his duties as a Mason. Through his support of the charities, particularly the Masonic Schools for the orphaned sons and daughters of Masons. In those days such children were supported through their school days by Masonic sponsorship.

He became a member of many Lodges, including the Grand Lodge of Great Britain which met in Queen Street, London. Ben would drive off into the night carrying his leather case, containing his apron, white gloves and little book of words. He found learning the ritual tiresome and many times I would have to listen and prompt him as he tried to remember the text.

Through his financial support and his commitment he reached a high rank in the world of Masonry, much of it a mystery to his family. I remember how my Granddad would tease him at every opportunity about Masonry,

"What ever do you see in that old squit? Bein' blind folded and pullin' up yore ruddy trouser leg" and he and Grace would laugh that their Bennie took it so seriously.

I think for my father, the 'Great Architect of the Universe' and the quiet services that Masonry gave to their poorer brothers, was Dad's main way of serving the Almighty. At heart he was an idealist and for the same reason was an advocate for the European Union, as a means of bringing together all the nations of Europe.

He would have been proud that his eldest grand daughter teaches at the Royal Masonic School for Girls in Rickmansworth.

When Twinings closed the Coffee Mill in Thetford, Ben proposed that Thet Lodge should buy it and convert it into a temple and refectory for the sole use of Lodge meetings, which were formerly in the Guildhall.

With his usual gusto he undertook the renovation single handed, with some assistance from Colonel Walter Short, another ardent Mason. Although my father was now nearing seventy he could still undertake heavy physical work.

When I went home for a visit he proudly showed me the refurbishments before it was officially opened;

"See the roof and the gold stars on the blue canopy of Heaven" he said.

A magical moment that reminded me of Yeats' poem,

"Had I the heaven's embroidered cloths

Enwrought with golden and silver light".

Although Ben belonged to Rotary for a number of years he felt that Rotary trumpeted its charitable deeds. He enjoyed the comradeship of fellow Rotarians but prized the religious aspects of Masonry and its stealth in giving, more than the much heralded deeds of Rotary.

He liked the inclusiveness of Masonry; that men from all faiths could join.

Ben had a Sikh friend, Suneet Bakhshi, in the Lion Lodge of Norwich and thinking of him, wrote this poem in 1994, at the time of conflict in the Balkans between Christians and Muslims.

Sarajevo we will save you
Sarajevo must not die
Stop cruel mortars, causing slaughter
Innocent children, mothers cry.
Blue capped UN come to help you
Come with love and not with hate
Entering your lovely city
Open now the final gate.
Masons help and send you aid
Not a debt that must be paid.
Our beliefs are answers to
Racial problems old and new,
Each brother worships as he pleases
Not confined by any creed
Masons believe a Supreme Being
and honest life in every deed.
Brotherly love is our tradition,
Christian, Muslim, Arab, Jew.
In Lion Lodge we meet Indians,
Also topped by heads in blue,
Suneet Bakhshi and his father
Beautiful turbans, lovely hue.
In Lodge we meet in harmony
All are equal, all are one
One day you must try it,
Sarajevo, it could save you
Peace must come
Instead of guns.

This poem, written when Ben was 86 years old, shows that he never lost his idealistic, optimistic view of the world.

Cynics might sneer and scoff that Ben had ulterior motives in being generous but the majority of people who met him and got to know him bore testimony to his good intentions.

It was not self promotion that earned him the title 'Mr Thetford' but the fact that he was genuinely liked and respected in the town.

Jessie and Ben, 'Mr Thetford', by the Tom Paine statue, King's Street, Thetford.

Chapter Thirty Five

Desperate Measures

One announcement my father had once made at 'Folly House' frightened me very much.

"Of course I'll probably drop dead of a heart attack when I'm fifty."

"Don't be soft, Bennie", his mother Grace replied,

"Just because you've got a lot of go in you, don't mean you won't last. Why, your grandfather John Chase had a hard life but he lived to a good 'ole age."

But the remark Daddy had made, slightly in jest, shocked me and I was fearful we might lose him.

Sturdily built and not afraid of tough physical work when it was needed, Ben Culey didn't drop dead at fifty. His heart was strong.

But another thing he said, to me when we were alone together, certainly came true.

He was sitting in one of the large, comfy chairs in the lounge, back lit by the afternoon sun shining in through the Art Deco style bow windows of 'Shrublands'.

"Anne, there's a saying 'from rags to riches and back in three generations' and the way things are going with me it's likely to be true."

I took this for the warning it was intended to be.

"Thank goodness I can support myself as a teacher" I remembered thinking. "At least I won't be reduced to 'rags'!"

Noting the unfortunate effect that comfortably placed parents could have on their children; for instance on the characters of Johnny, Edna and Willie; my parents had always been determined that I should make my own way in life.

The farms had failed, Hanbury's garage had become Nice's garage because of Ben's frustration. Later the land on which it stood had been bought by McCarthy and Stone, who built apartments.

The restaurant and the milk bar had been sold because they lost money.

207

Ben enjoyed setting up a new venture but if it became troublesome, he then tired of it, wanting to move on to another project. However, whenever he needed capital there was always something he could sell to free up some cash, for he also owned a fair amount of property in Thetford.

Now he was beginning to realise he would have to make changes.

He talked things over with Jessie.

"I think we ought to think about sizing down Jessie, 'Shrublands' is getting a bit too big for us two."

There had been a lavish wedding reception for Jeffrey, my husband and I, in 1960, to which 250 people were invited. Ben was up into the small hours concocting one large bowl of alcoholic punch and one non-alcoholic punch for the teetotallers. Unfortunately at the wedding the servers muddled them up and some abstemious Methodists returned home rather more happily than usual, after imbibing the wrong punch!

Jessie had long realised they couldn't go on in such style but she firmly resisted Ben's first plan to divide 'Shrublands' into two, renting out one half of it for income. "I don't want other people living in our house" she said, recalling how many people they had had to accommodate during the war.

Ben drew up plans for a bungalow in the extensive grounds of Shrublands. In true Culey fashion the plans were extended and another storey added.

Building began, Ben joining in the labouring work with gusto. Everything was of the best quality, deep concrete foundations, Tomo windows, a Baxi fireplace and a glass brick window the length of the stair well. The bathrooms included not only showers but bidets and the downstairs rooms had modern wood panelling in the Swedish style.

Plans for budgeting flew out of the large picture windows. A swimming pool was constructed. 'for the grand daughters'.

The finished house was almost as big as Shrublands and the sale of the first 'Shrublands', to be named 'Riversmeet,' didn't cover the expense of building the second house.

Ben and Jessie moved in 1964 and Margot and Keith Eldred came to live in 'Riversmeet'. Mark and Richard, their sons, grew up to enjoy the house and gardens as much as Anne had done. In the same spirit as in

Ben and Jessie's time there was much entertaining. To count Margot and Keith as friends is a joy, for I can still visit my old home.

Ben and Jessie's three little grand daughters looked forward to visiting Thetford.

As soon as the car drew near Elveden I would say,

"Wind down the car windows and smell the fresh, clean country air," because the girls were growing up in the polluted air of south east London.

During the 1970s Ben decided the cinema was in need of refurbishment and thought it would bring in more trade if it was modernised, so he introduced a side entrance, positioned a sweet and cigarette venue to the left, which was named the Candy Box and to the front where the cashier used to sit, was now a shop. At first this was a delicatessen, John Chase, Ben's second cousin, came over from Lynn to set it up, but, when that didn't go well it became a toy and fancy goods emporium.

'Anne's', Jessie's emporium.

Jessie was involved in the ordering and when a shop became available on King Street the business was moved there. It was named 'Anne's', with my handwritten signature as the shop front sign. It was next to Aubyn Davies the gentleman's outfitters.

Strangely, although she was nearly seventy, Jessie was proud to have her own gift shop business and would go to the shop daily. She had the help of one assistant, and ordered goods with her innate good taste. She also displayed them attractively and with imagination.

I think she was pleased to be able to help Ben with his financial difficulties and the little shop was a success, although it became too much for Jessie to handle on a daily basis, as she grew older.

Unfortunately, trying to pay off loans on the new 'Shrublands 'and keeping the overheads down on house and garden became too expensive, despite Jessie's efforts at 'Annes'.

The refurbished cinema was not bringing in the customers; though it had opened with the usual Culey flourish of a free show and refreshments. Most people soon returned to the Odeon at Bury St Edmunds, which could easily be reached by bus or by the increasingly available private car. Bury was only twelve miles away.

The large cinema chains were still able to bargain for the latest films more successfully than small independent cinemas.

"We're going to have to move from here," Ben admitted to Jessie, "I can't make ends meet."

"Oh Ben, no."

A very unhappy Jessie was overwhelmed at the thought of moving again.

So in their seventies Ben and Jessie sadly had to leave 'Shrublands 2'.

I tried to suggest ways in which they could budget, for I had learnt to live more frugally as a Minister's wife. I explained that they didn't need magazine subscriptions, or the paper delivered daily, or to give donations to so many good causes because it was 'expected of them' but my advice fell on deaf ears; maybe because they'd become so used to living in a certain style?

In desperation Daddy told me,

"I'd get a job as a tractor driver if anyone would have me"

At his age this was unlikely.

Shortly afterwards they moved to Nunnery Drive, a new development that had been built close to Barnham Common.

They were so dispirited that Ben left behind shed loads of china and glass from the failed Anglian cafe.

No 7, Nunnery Drive was a fair sized house. The house appealed because there was a swimming pool in the back garden for his granddaughters' visits.

Jessie, as ever, was good at adapting and making a house a home.

In 1980 Ben and Jessie celebrated their Golden Wedding, once more inviting a large number of guests to a meal and musical entertainment in the Carnegie rooms. at the Guildhall. Ben was on fine form, catching Jessie round the waist and kissing her as he swung her round in a waltz.

"The best thing I ever done was to pay 7/6d for a wedding licence. Why, you can't even buy a birthday card at that price now!" he said in his speech.

"That was the best 7/6d worth I ever spent" he quipped, his blue eyes twinkling as he winked at his audience.

"The flower arrangements on the tables are for the ladies. I hope you'll take them home," he added.

I didn't really know how impoverished my parents were when they treated their many guests to this lavish entertainment.

Soon they were having to face another 'downsize' as financial pressures forced them to move to a house in Canons Close in 1982. Once there Jessie fretted that it was;

"On the wrong side of Thetford."

Canons Close was situated on the far side of the town's ring road. As it was a north facing house, with a depressingly concreted garden, it was probably these factors that were the main reason why my mother never 'settled' there.

Their last move was to an end of terrace house in Norfolk Road facing Melford Common.

Because of the open outlook, Jessie, who suffered from claustrophobia, was much happier. Every day she enjoyed watching people walking their dogs across the Common.

Ben, of course, was not content until he'd put his mark on the little house. This consisted of wood panelling in the living room, to act as sound proofing from the house next door. He also began a downstairs extension but by now the money had completely run out and the workmen flatly refused to continue building. The unfinished toilet stood as a constant reminder of their impoverished situation.

To occupy his mind Ben took up 'comping,' which is entering competitons in magazines and newspapers, always with the hope of winning some big prize.

This never came his way but he was successful in winning a holiday in Zell-am-See, Austria, from a Delmonte tinned fruit offer and a few days in Copenhagen from a Danepak competition. His little 'office' in the third bedroom was crammed to overflowing with the wrappers and goods he'd had to buy, in order to take part in competitions.

Then the medication he was prescribed for diabetes slowed him up at last. His speech became laboured and he grew lethargic.

David Osborne, Thetford's historian, interviewed him and a film was made entitled 'Ben Culey's Thetford'. It distressed me to hear his slow, laboured speech on the sound track.

He had once been so quick witted, so alert.

The next door neighbour phoned me,

"Anne, I'm worried. Your Dad isn't getting about. He just sits in his chair all day, staring out of the window."

I didn't guess how severely depressed he'd become, for he always put on a good face when we visited,

"Your mother and I don't eat like this all the time you know, only when you visit," he'd say as we tucked into the prawn cocktails he'd made.

I thought this was just banter, I didn't know that he had re-mortgaged the house and was unable to keep up with the payments.

One night the telephone's piercing tones awoke me at 2 o'clock in the morning, according to the alarm clock by my bed. Still befuddled by sleep I tried to clear my head and listen. It was Dad's Building Society.

"Your father owes us a lot of money. What are you going to do about it? Do you think your father's a victim? We are the 'victims' because he isn't paying back money he owes us!"

The angry voice carried on for several minutes, whilst I tried to make sense of it all.

The assault went on for several nights, at two or three o'clock in the morning, to jolt me awake and frighten me.

I protested that I wasn't in a position to clear his debts. I had no idea that he had got into arrears and that the interest had piled up so frighteningly.

Then my parents were sent a letter threatening them with eviction.

An eighty five year old couple were to be turned onto the street. The amount owed by my father had got to a staggering amount because of the interest accruing on the unpaid monthly sums.

After years of Ben supporting Masonic charities with big donations, I thought the Masons would help him in his hour of need and offer my parents a place at Cornwallis Court in Bury St Edmunds, a residential home for elderly Masons.

My father, some years earlier, had helped in the negotiations to purchase the property and land, on behalf of the Masonic Order.

The well placed Masons I spoke to by 'phone were tough; believing that my father must have hidden assets. He had been so generous towards Masonry in the past. They could not believe he was destitute and therefore they were loathe to help. Indeed they pressed me, thinking I would reveal where his money was. It was only after I angrily complained to a senior member of Masonry,

"You were ready to take his money but you'll turn your back on him now he has nothing."

Then I continued and I could feel my temper rising,

"I think it's all a load of hooey anyway. Perhaps the national press will be interested to hear about this. My parents are to be be turned out of their home in a fortnight's time and you are no longer interested in helping 'poor and distressed Masons, wheresoever they may be'. I know that all Masons say this as a tenet; setting out your beliefs. I used to help my father learn the ritual."

Finally, with the help of a few loyal Masonic friends, two single rooms were suddenly conveniently 'available' at Cornwallis Court.

With the help of a friend's van we packed some essential belongings. I drove my mother over to Bury St Edmunds. She was traumatised and didn't utter one word on that fateful journey. But neither did the stoical Jessie cry, for which I was grateful.

I had to take time off work to clear the little house, salvaging what we could, selling other things and making many journeys to the town refuse site, before the house was peremptorily taken over by the Building Society and quickly sold for the paltry amount of £35,000.

It would have fetched much more if it had been sold by an estate agent.

When the management of Cornwallis Court realised that they would receive nothing of the proceeds of this sale, they were furious and again my parents faced the prospect of eviction.

Only when they realised that they could at least recoup money from the back payments Ben should have claimed from Social Security, did they speak to my elderly parents, who were summoned, like naughty children, to Matron's office, where a senior administrator was waiting to harangue them.

My mother was so upset she said,

"I have never been treated like this in my life and I'm not having it now,"

Then she left the room. How I admired her for keeping her dignity!

Meanwhile my father continued to be rebuked;

"Well, you can stay, but you must give up your stereo set for the common good".

It was placed in the residents' lounge but disappeared mysteriously after a few months.

Finally my parents were given a double room facing out across trees towards Hardwicke Heath.

Cornwallis Court was formerly the Bristol Annexe, where Daddy had had his infected appendix removed fifty years before.

Fortunately they settled down well to life in the Home as they had always been sociable souls. When visitors called, Jessie would hurry to the little kitchen and get out the china tea set, drape a white cloth over the small all-purpose table and serve tea and biscuits. Her high standards never slipped, even when most of the cups and saucers had become chipped, for elderly hands become stiff and clumsy in managing delicate objects.

"Look at them," Dad would remark, as the elderly residents slowly shuffled along the passage to the dining room, holding carefully onto the rails on each side of the passage.

"It's just like rush hour on the M25!"

He had regained his impish sense of humour since the medication for his diabetes had been reduced in strength.

Determined to keep independent and not institutionalised, Jessie would put her coat and hat on and sally forth every afternoon for her 'constitutional' walk, come rain or shine.

"Oh you're not going out in this weather, Jessie," the more delicate inhabitants would say but Jessie just kept on walking.

Sometimes Ben would forget he and Jessie were only allowed £14 'pocket money' per week for small items. Once he hired a taxi to take them to Wells -next- the Sea and back,

"Because Jessie really needed the sea air"

"But I would have taken you, Daddy," was my response.

How he hated being dependent on others!

On several occasions I had to phone local businesses and cancel orders for mobility scooters or reclining chairs. Obviously Dad couldn't have paid for them. He was also in the habit of getting staff to buy him a £10 lottery ticket, in the hopes that he would land a big win. He'd forgotten his former antipathy towards gambling.

"Oh, you are a cruel girl," he would complain, when I refused to indulge him. I disapproved of the lottery, still remembering what Percy's gambling did to my Aunt Edna. Now that Mummy could only afford clothes from Charity Shops and needed new stockings, even £10 a week on a lottery ticket was beyond their means, and I resented Daddy frittering away such a meagre sum because it left Mummy short of her 'pocket money'.

It was a sad time for the family, despite their resilience. At the same time I was relieved that my parents were in safe hands. I knew my parents were well cared for and were liked by the very competent staff of the Home, for their health was gradually declining.

Ben has a road named after him in Thetford.

Chapter Thirty Six

The Curtain Falls

"Time, like an ever rolling stream
Bears all its sons away,
They fly, forgotten, as a dream
Dies at the break of day" - **Isaac Watts**

It is late October 1998 and I am preparing tea in my carrstone cottage at Heacham. Soon my husband will be bringing Mummy and Aunt Cassie to see it for the first time. By now Daddy needed a wheelchair and assistance, so he wasn't coming today. Suddenly the telephone rings.

"Hello, is that Mrs Bloomfield?" I can hear one of the kind Philippino staff on the line.

"This is one of the nurses at Cornwallis Court. In the present circumstances we don't think it wise for your mother to come out today."

'The circumstances' were tiredness and breathlessness.

A fortnight later, Mummy had a stroke. As she waited for the ambulance I sat with her and held her frail hand. She mouthed a message to me,

"Sing to me, Anne."

I recalled those journeys back from Lynn on starry nights, the rugs around our knees. Motor cars didn't have heating in those days. Happily we sang songs from musical shows to while away the miles.

"When the sun in the morning creeps over the hill
and wakens the roses on my windowsill."

As I sang 'Mocking Bird Hill', one of Mummy's favourites, she managed a lopsided smile and tapped her hand to the tune.

The stay in hospital was a nightmare. A worse stroke had followed and she could only manage liquids. Then it became 'nil by mouth' and she was fed intravenously. Mummy grew thinner and weaker and a nurse told me,

"It's just a holding process now."

I pleaded that she be allowed to return home to Cornwallis Court.

Another, more callous nurse commented,

"I don't think they'll want her back in this state."

Fortunately the staff at the Cornwallis Court were more compassionate and on the last day of her life, Mummy was taken back to loving surroundings, where Daddy could be wheeled to sit with her.

On a crisp frosty morning, December 6th, 1998, Jessie Maud Mabel Culey passed away. Somehow it was appropriate that she, who had grown up in St Nicholas House, opposite St Nicholas Chapel, should die on St Nicholas' day.

We waited until her eldest grand daughter Rachel had booked a flight from Australia, so that she could be with us for the funeral.

Rachel, Emma and Rebecca, her loving grand-daughters, were able to hold in check their emotions and spoke at the service.

Next day we laid some of the flowers in Thetford Forest, where Jessie loved to picnic, we took some to her old home at St Nicholas House, where the solicitors staff were surprised but pleased to receive them and the last flowers we threw into the cold tide at Hunstanton, which was the holiday resort where she'd spent many happy seaside times with her mother and father, sisters and brother.

That Christmas I could not bear the usual bright Christmas decorations but only white or green.

On Christmas Day we were touched that my Father came with little presents wrapped in paper napkins; small gifts for everyone, even though he was very lost without his Jessie. He'd retained his impulse for generosity.

He had been moved to a single room and he carried on, enjoying his days out with the family and a visit to Thetford's Mayoral celebrations, where he managed a long day without a hint of being tired.

Having retired three years earlier, I had booked for a 'Big Overseas Experience' as New Zealanders term it when they travel around the world. Mine would begin with a flight to Los Angeles, California, so that I could see Dad's beloved Hollywood for myself.

When I visited Cornwallis Court to be with Dad for a while before I set off on my adventure, I had every hope of seeing him again on my return.

Yet as left, I heard him calling after me, in a strangely sad way, as I began to walk down the corridor.

"Goodbye Anne, goodbye, goodbye." It was a cry from the heart. I hurried back and gave him another big hug.

Did he sense that he wouldn't see me again? Who knows?

On a bright September afternoon a ferry took me across the beautiful Straits that divide the North and South Islands of New Zealand. Little did I know that my father was dying as I took that journey.

I caught the train to Christchurch, where one of Rachel's former boyfriends, also called Ben, met me and took me home to meet his wife. After dinner we relaxed with our glasses of wine. Suddenly the telephone rang in Ben's study. He answered it and said,

"Anne, it's Jeffrey on the phone for you."

I hurried through to the other room. International calls cost a lot of money.

"Hello Anne," Jeffrey began "You'd better sit down."

It was then I knew what he was going to say. Being told to 'sit down' ready to receive some news is never a good sign. I knew before he spoke another word that Daddy had died.

Jeffrey said,

"The General" (for that's what Jeff affectionately called my father) "died last night. He had a massive stroke." Jeff continued,

"Matthew at Cornwallis Court phoned yesterday and asked me to go over. He said your father hadn't been feeling well. I took Rebecca with me.

We had a good evening together. Your Dad chatted about various events in his life. Then he summed it all up by saying;

'I've had a good life and I don't regret a thing.'

When we left he held onto my hand and I said to him,

'You know General, you've taken me to places and given me experiences I could never have had but for your generosity.'

Then Rebecca and I left and his great domed head sank back peacefully onto the pillows."

I was pleased to hear from Jeff that Dad had shown him the card he'd received that very morning. I'd sent it from Hollywood. It showed the

219

famous sign high on the Hollywood Hills. How I wish he could have seen it for himself. But for Daddy, knowing I had been there; that would have been the next best thing.

Ben was released from his wheel chair, from the indignities of old age, from the loneliness of losing Jessie.

Although he was a very public man, who had boundless energy and enjoyed the company of others, it was the family man who taught me to row a boat, to ride a bike, to stay on a pony, to paint and to be independent. More than these things, I have benefitted all my life from his insatiable curiosity, his zest for life, his optimistic outlook, his sense of fun and his penchant for puns, that great hearty laugh and his generous spirit.

Ben – showing his sense of fun

Epilogue

It is October 2001. The leaves are falling from the trees that line the path of Spring Walks in Thetford.

A small group of people composed of our family, a couple of friends, two Council dignitaries and two Council employees, are gathered on the banks of the River Thet, at the spot where it flows into the Little Ouse.

I am shivering although it is not cold, indeed it is a mild, sunny morning.

In my hand I hold a spade that feels too heavy to lift. I look for support to my husband, standing at the side of me but I get no response. His face is set; it is his way of coping.

The two council men stand ready. Their black coats are sombre and this makes me more sorrowful.

I try to lift the spade but I can't manage it and one of the men comes forward. He sees that I'm shaking and he takes the spade from me.

Swiftly and strongly the hole is dug. About eighteen inches deep and square. I open the metal cannister and shake it. The fine dust is blown sideways by a sudden breeze and I am fearful it will settle in the wrong place.

I struggle with the words that I've chosen for the committal of my parents' ashes,

"Take them earth for cherishing

Receive them to thy tender breast,"

from the 'Hymnus Paradisi' song of the Earth, set to music by Herbert Howells.

I'm trying hard not to cry.

One of the officials brings forward the young plane tree sapling and places it in position. The dust has settled into the moist rich earth.

Ben and Jessie's ashes are laid to rest close to the place so dear to them.

Their epitaph mentions how Ben was known as 'Mr Thetford,' of how he was elected Mayor three times, of how they loved and promoted their town.

"But life that keep a'goin' on
   And the best thing we can do
   Is call to mind his friendly humorous words,
   Ah, you and me and several more
   Have got a lot to thank him for
   We've lost a good old friend, I reckon, Bor,
   For he won't take any pictures any more." - Attributed to 'John Kett'

Ben and Jessie on one of their last outings together.

The Family Tree

*People mentioned in this book

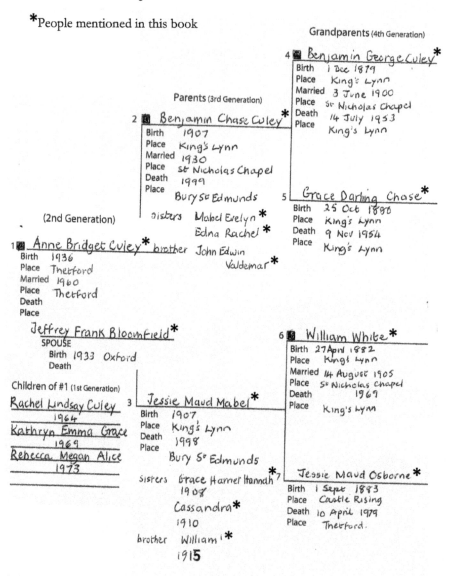

Grandparents (4th Generation)

4 Benjamin George Culey*
Birth 1 Dec 1879
Place King's Lynn
Married 3 June 1900
Place St Nicholas Chapel
Death 14 July 1953
Place King's Lynn

Parents (3rd Generation)

2 Benjamin Chase Culey*
Birth 1907
Place King's Lynn
Married 1930
Place St Nicholas Chapel
Death 1999
Place Bury St Edmunds

sisters Mabel Evelyn*
Edna Rachel*

5 Grace Darling Chase*
Birth 25 Oct 1880
Place King's Lynn
Death 9 Nov 1954
Place King's Lynn

(2nd Generation)

1 Anne Bridget Culey* brother John Edwin Valdemar*
Birth 1936
Place Thetford
Married 1960
Place Thetford
Death
Place

Jeffrey Frank Bloomfield*
SPOUSE
Birth 1933 Oxford
Death

6 William White*
Birth 27 April 1882
Place King's Lynn
Married 14 August 1905
Place St Nicholas Chapel
Death 1969
Place King's Lynn

Children of #1 (1st Generation)

Rachel Lindsay Culey
1964
Kathryn Emma Grace
1969
Rebecca Megan Alice
1973

3 Jessie Maud Mabel*
Birth 1907
Place King's Lynn
Death 1998
Place Bury St Edmunds

sisters Grace Harriet Hannah*
1908
Cassandra*
1910
brother William*
1915

7 Jessie Maud Osborne*
Birth 1 Sept 1883
Place Castle Rising
Death 10 April 1979
Place Thetford.

224

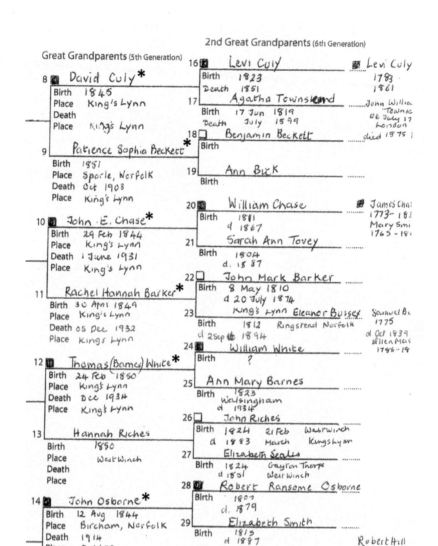

16 Levi Culy
Birth 1823
Death 1851

Levi Culy
1783
1861

8 David Culy *
Birth 1845
Place King's Lynn
Death
Place King's Lynn

17 Agatha Townsend
Birth 17 Jun 1819
Death July 1899

John Willia
Townse
06 July 17
London
died 1875 1

18 Benjamin Beckett
Birth

9 Patience Sophia Beckett *
Birth 1851
Place Sporle, Norfolk
Death Oct 1903
Place King's Lynn

19 Ann Bick
Birth

20 William Chase
Birth 1811
d 1867

James Chas
1773- 18
Mary Smi
1765 - 18

10 John E. Chase *
Birth 29 Feb 1844
Place King's Lynn
Death 1 June 1931
Place King's Lynn

21 Sarah Ann Tovey
Birth 1804
d. 1887

22 John Mark Barker
Birth 8 May 1810
d 20 July 1874
King's Lynn

11 Rachel Hannah Barker *
Birth 30 April 1849
Place King's Lynn
Death 05 Dec 1932
Place Kings Lynn

23 Eleanor Bussey
Birth 1812 Ringstead Norfolk
d 2 Sep 1894

Samuel B
1775
d Oct 1839
Ellen Mas
1786 - 19

24 William White
Birth ?

12 Thomas (Barnes) White *
Birth 24 Feb 1850
Place King's Lynn
Death Dec 1934
Place King's Lynn

25 Ann Mary Barnes
Birth 1823
Walsingham
d 1934

26 John Riches
Birth 1824 21 Feb Westwinch
d 1883 March Kingshyam

13 Hannah Riches
Birth 1850
Place West Winch
Death
Place

27 Elizabeth Scales
Birth 1824 Gayton Thorpe
d 1851 West Winch

28 Robert Ransome Osborne
Birth 1807
d. 1879

14 John Osborne *
Birth 12 Aug 1844
Place Bircham, Norfolk
Death 1914
Place Docking

29 Elizabeth Smith
Birth 1815
d 1887

30 John Hill
Birth 1815
d. 1896

Robert Hill
b 1757 Flit
d 1829 Bin

15 Harriet Hill
Birth 7 Dec 1845
Place Gt Bircham
Death 1908
Place Gt Bircham

31 Jemima Suckling *
Birth 26 Sept 1819